To
John
All the best

Brent

Praise for The People-Profit Connection

"Brent's enormously readable book demystifies the concept of emotional intelligence and links people skills and success in the construction industry-in fact, in any industry. A definite "must read".
—Lisa Fanto, Senior Vice President,
Corporate and Communication Services, Hardin Construction

"We believe that relationships are our greatest asset. Brent's book takes this central idea, practically applies the concept of emotional intelligence, and offers real solutions to many industry problems. I would recommend it to any construction professional."
—Jim Griffin, CEO, R.J. Griffin & Company

"Construction has always been a people business, but the human resource challenges of the new millennium have industry players scrambling like never before to capture and utilize talent. Brent Darnell has produced a great handbook for anyone in the construction industry who wishes to elevate their understanding of the human dimension."
—Hank Harris, President, FMI Corporation

"Brent's book on the *The People-Profit Connection* has been well received by our managers; they describe it as "on target" for our industry. We use emotional intelligence concepts to support our talent management work, and this book is particularly helpful in making the ideas practical in their application: better relationships produce better business outcomes."
—Dr. Pam Mayer, Succession & Development Manager,
Granite Construction Inc.

"You hit the nail on the head."
—Dr. Wayne Clough, President, Georgia Institute of Technology

"Your observations and case studies reinforce our thinking about the next level of skill development we have identified. The methodology you outlined incorporating an emotional intelligence perspective is great input as we work to elevate our peoples' skills, business success, and, ultimately, client satisfaction."
—Mary C. Bloom, Corporate Director of Client Satisfaction,
Gilbane Building Company

"Brent Darnell's book provides a critical link to creating high performing and motivated teams by helping us understand Emotional Intelligence. It will help you to create a climate where you can articulate a shared mission that moves people and, ultimately, create successful projects."

—Bruce D'Agostino, Executive Director
Construction Management Association of America

"Every developer needs to read this little book. Recognizing that our emotional skills control our behavior, Brent identifies the key to great success – care as much about the needs of your team as your own - it's just too simple to be wrong and it applies to so much more than business."

—Lou Conti, VP – Development, Cousins Properties Incorporated

"Brent Darnell has taken on the most difficult task of helping the construction industry realize their opportunities to re-invent their sector, utilizing emotional intelligence. Brent, I applaud your efforts to help the happiness quotient of our partners in the built environment."

—Joyce LaValle, Sr. Vice President of Human Services,
InterfaceFLOR Commercial

"Brent Darnell's book makes a very subtle but dramatic point – emotional intelligence is revelant to performance in every job and any industry! He offers compelling stories and powerful insights. The book is full of ideas for improving individual and organizational performance by tapping the power of emotion."

—Kate Cannon, EQ Pioneer

"Brent Darnell's book accurately depicts the construction industry's reality and its need to change. More importantly, it identifies the emotional skills required to be successful in changing the industry and provides a direction in which the industry must go. In my opinion, without a focus on emotional intelligence, the industry will continue on a slow decline."

—Joe Andronaco, President, USA Technology Services

"Brent Darnell breaks down the most complicated part of our business – the human psyche – into useable and quantifiable steps in *The People-Profit Connection*. The process of placing people in the right positions, and training employees to enhance their people-skills is simplified by using emotional intelligence. This leads to a Win-Win situation with happier employees and better company margins. What more could anyone ask for?"

—Rick Alcala, Construction Consultant, zumBrunnen, Inc.

"Brent's book is a good example for all the companies which want to be better. It shows in a very understandable way how companies can change just by paying REAL attention to their people, the only possible way to be different to become the best."

—Josep Sala i Teixidó, sales manager Spain, Greece, Latin America, Poggenpohl Möbelwerke GmbH (A member of the Nobia group)

"Mr. Darnell's book deftly explains the complex psychological factors that govern personal relationships in a simple set of readily understandable layman's terms called "Emotional Intelligence." It shows how improving these people skills at every personnel level affects business performance in intuitively obvious, but often overlooked, ways. I recommend it to anyone interested in smooth, safe, and profitable construction."

—Bailey Pope, AIA, VP Design and Construction, Harold A Dawson Company

"The book is a gem! Easy to read and understand, practical and hands-on."

—Margareta Sjölund, PhD, founder of Kandidata

"I believe there is a great deal of substance in the approach to utilizing emotional intelligence as a basis to bring about positive changes in Construction Professionals."

—Tracy MacDonald, Project Director, McCarthy Construction

"*The People-Profit Connection* is a great read. In this concise and candid book, Brent Darnell sets out a method for improving construction company job performance by developing a better understanding of both our co-workers and ourselves."

—Robyn E. Ice, Partner, Rosenberg & Estis

THE
PEOPLE-PROFIT
CONNECTION

THE
PEOPLE-PROFIT
CONNECTION

HOW EMOTIONAL INTELLIGENCE
CAN MAXIMIZE PEOPLE SKILLS
& MAXIMIZE YOUR
PROFITS

G. Brent Darnell

SWEET TEA PUBLISHERS · ATLANTA

Dedication

This book is dedicated to my parents:

Bob Darnell,
the builder of bridges between people and places,
who taught me how to get along
with my fellow man,

and Betty Darnell,
the life of the party,
who never met a
stranger.

Contents

Acknowledgements

I want to thank my wife, Andrea, for all of her encouragement and support. My appreciation also goes to Kate Cannon for her right-on comments, mentoring, and friendship. Hats off to Diana Durek and all of the folks at Multi-Health Systems, Inc., Margareta Sjölund at Kandidata for introducing me to emotional intelligence, Pat Dunwoody of the Associated Builders and Contractors for all of her early help and validation, Geetu Bharwaney for her insightful feedback, Pam Pate, the editing guru, and all of the other kind readers who have given me great suggestions and advice. I also want to extend a big thanks to all of the participants from these courses who have started their journey toward personal mastery. Thanks also go to the individuals and companies who took the leap of faith and embraced this work, especially Lisa Fanto and all of the gracious folks at Hardin Construction. To those companies who have agreed to share their case studies, I am eternally grateful. And finally, a huge thanks to Ed Legum for all of his help in turning this book into a reality.

Foreword to the Second Edition
By Gary Draper, Draper & Associates

When robots and black boxes build projects, we won't need Brent Darnell's advice anymore. Until then, however, we need to pay close attention to what he has to say.

Brent's systematic take on the concept of emotional intelligence is not only worth looking into, it also compels us to explore that mysterious region of the project business: the people jungle. It's gotten too expensive to play ostrich when people problems infect the project team.

Brent's approach can help each of us to know that:

- We have a people problem.
- We can isolate the cause of the problem.
- We can help fix the problem.

It's true – people can change, and change for the better. And applying emotional intelligence techniques can facilitate that change.

Brent has three histories going for him:

1. Brent learned his first lessons from his dad, Bob Darnell. Bob's a real leader in the construction business in helping people solve their problems using the personal approach. I know because I learned a lot from Bob, too.

2. Brent's in-the-field experience. He's been immersed in the school of hard knocks.

3. Brent's professional experience in applying emotional intelligence for a multitude of clients.

Dig in, and you will gain new insights into getting things done in our people-driven world.

Introduction

Innovation is more than a new method. It is a new view of the universe, as one of risk rather than of chance or of certainty. It is a new view of man's role in the universe; he creates order by taking risks. And this means that innovation, rather than being an assertion of human power, is an acceptance of human responsibility.
—Peter Drucker

God gave us so many emotions, and so many strong ones. Every human being, even if he is an idiot, is a millionaire in emotions.
—Isaac Bashevis Singer

When the human species has learned to harness emotion, we will be ready to take the next evolutionary step.
—Charles Darwin

This book was written specifically for the construction industry, but the more I talked to people outside of the construction industry, the more they confirmed that these issues were applicable to many businesses. This is especially true of service industries where the employees are technically educated or trained, such as engineering, healthcare, legal, information technology, telecommunications, manufacturing, finance, and accounting. They all have similar problems that relate directly to their collaborative, service oriented nature and the employees' need to effectively deal with people. By addressing these people issues, organizations can be transformed, become less problematic, and add more to their bottom lines. In fact, if these concepts work for the construction industry, which is generally slow to embrace change, they will work for any industry.

Imagine for a moment a brilliant future for the construction industry where highly respected managers balance their toughness, assertiveness, and independence with highly effective interpersonal skills. Imagine an industry that is completely service oriented and customer focused, with zero defects and total customer satisfaction. Imagine an industry where there is trust, communication, and teamwork among the owners, construction managers, architects, designers, contractors, subcontractors, vendors, and suppliers. Imagine an industry where all projects are completed ahead of schedule and well within the budget, where negotiated contracts are the norm, where employees are respected and encouraged to thrive, where productivity skyrockets, and profit margins increase dramatically. Imagine an industry where sustainable construction is the norm, where the industry's processes not only do no harm, but also contribute to a healthier planet. Consider the power of communication and teamwork so widespread that project teams love to come to work each morning, where relationships are so strong and concern for others is so pervasive that people look out for each other and working safely is as natural as breathing. Imagine an industry that draws millions of young men and women because they want to be a part of this wonderful business, to work together to build something, to create something from nothing. That is the industry I want to be a part of, that is waiting to be.

But the big question is, "Why isn't the industry like that now?" It's a very good question that deserves an answer. In fact, that is the purpose of this book – to determine how the industry can transform itself into the one I have just described. There are many seemingly unsolvable problems that prevent us from having such an industry. I'm sure you are thinking of those problems right now. The first step toward solving these complex issues is to find their root causes. Once we do that, we can begin to find solutions.

I have asked successful construction people about these industry problems and have heard many different responses, but the common denominator seems to be related to difficulties with people. One person joked, "If it weren't for the people, this would be a fun business." When construction professionals were asked where they spend the majority of their time, they replied, "Dealing with people problems." We all know that this is a difficult industry made more complicated by the myriad of problems associated with this human dimension, which probably goes back to the building of the pyramids. The dilemma is that no one has come up with an effective way to solve these people problems – until now.

This book explores the most difficult construction industry problems, provides some insight into their root causes, and shows how to go about solving them. And when your company solves these problems, your bottom line will dramatically increase. In order to address people issues, it is logical that we examine the people. That is where emotional intelligence comes in. What is emotional intelligence? One simple definition is "social competence". It includes cultivating a level of personal mastery, which enables you to deal more effectively with others. This can be a difficult but worthwhile process. As Lao Tzu said, "Mastering others is strength. Mastering yourself makes you fearless." Using emotional intelligence as a foundation, we have found a way to measure and improve people skills and solve people-related problems. Teaching people skills to contractors using emotional intelligence is the basis of our business.

At the beginning of this journey, when I told my wife I was going to teach emotional intelligence to contractors, she said I was crazy. How in the world could I teach these tough construction managers about emotional intelligence? Even I had my doubts. How would they react to learning about their own emotions and the emotions of others? The initial reactions, which are now predictable, were apprehension, skepticism, and resistance. But once these initial reactions were overcome, and participants realized that this emotional intelligence work was something that could be quite important for their career development and personal lives, virtually all of them embraced the concept. And once they embraced the concept and worked on their emotional intelligence, the results were nothing short of remarkable. As one participant put it, "I was apprehensive about this type of training in the beginning. However, after completing the course and seeing my own personal growth, I realize that the effort given has netted significant results." Another participant said, "There were times when I felt like the Karate Kid. I kept asking myself, 'why am I continuing to 'wax on, wax off'?' But in the end, the lessons really paid off."

This focus on the people side of business is nothing new. The introduction to Dale Carnegie's How to Win Friends and Influence People, which was published in 1936, states:

"Research done a few years ago under the auspices of the Carnegie Foundation for the Advancement of Teaching uncovered a most important and significant fact – a fact later confirmed by additional studies made at the Carnegie Institute of Technology. These investigations revealed that even in such technical lines as engineering, about fifteen percent of one's financial success is due to one's technical knowledge and about eighty-five percent is due to skill in human engineering – to personality and the ability to lead people."[1]

When I first started working with emotional intelligence, my skeptical engineer's brain had many questions. You will likely have similar questions and challenges as well. This book will answer your questions and give you a path to follow. We will discuss the basics of emotional intelligence and why it is vital to the future success of your company. By using the methodology outlined in this book, you will be able to measure and improve your employees' people skills, solve the industry problems, and eventually increase your bottom line.

1 : *An Introduction to Emotional Intelligence*

*People do not remember you by any intellectual idea
or concept you may have given them, but by some subtle
emotional impression you may have made consciously or
unconsciously. It is what one thinks about you
after you have left him that counts.*

—Frances Wilshire

WHAT MAKES A GREAT LEADER? Think for a moment about a great leader whom you admire, someone you really look up to. What are the characteristics that make this person great? Whenever I ask this question, I usually get a long list of skills. A great leader has good communication skills, empathy, listening skills, passion, assertiveness, focus, decisiveness, motivation skills, relationship skills, and vision. Invariably, it is a long list of the so-called "soft" skills, or emotional intelligence competencies. Very rarely does anyone say that a great leader has incredible technical skill or vast intellect or an advanced degree from a prestigious college.

Isn't this list of attributes just as valid for most areas of the construction business? Think of the best owner's representative, the best architect, the best designer, the best construction manager, the best laborer, the best carpenter, the best plumber, the best electrician, the best superintendent, or the best project manager. Don't most of them possess good people skills? Aren't these people skills a vital part of what makes them effective and what makes you want to work with them? Don't we continually receive requests for our best people, the ones who have those great interpersonal skills? Isn't it a shame that we can't put them on all of our projects? If people skills differentiate these stars, then why don't we try to cultivate these skills in all of our employees?

Most of our decisions are based on emotional responses. Most choices we make, the red Mustang, the dark woman with red hair, that favorite pair of blue jeans, even something as simple as how you like your eggs are triggered by emotional impulses. In fact, recent brain research reveals that the emotional part of the brain is involved in every aspect of our day-to-day thought processes. Without this connection to the emotional part of the brain, cognitive thought processes such as decision making are nearly impossible. Simply put, our brains are hardwired for emotion. We can't escape it. The limbic system, or the primitive, emotional center of our brain, is working all of the time.

There is an interesting case study in the book, Emotional Intelligence, by Daniel Goleman, a leader in this field. He tells us about Elliot, a successful lawyer, whose brain was damaged during an operation. The area that was damaged was the part of the brain that links the emotional part to the thinking part. Although he was cognitively intelligent, because he could not call upon the emotional part of his brain, he functioned more like a computer. As a result, his life fell apart. "He could no longer hold a job. His wife left him. Squandering his savings on fruitless investments, he was reduced to living in a spare bedroom in his brother's home." 2 Without this emotional link, the thinking brain could no longer assign values to the situations that arose. According to Goleman, "every option was neutral".

The people who study emotional intelligence began by asking a very simple, but profound question: What makes people successful? They tried to quantify it. They looked at IQ and other intelligence indicators. They looked at higher learning and technical training. Did success lie in having the best education? What about MBAs, PhDs and other postgraduate degrees? Did they give people the competitive edge to become more successful?

Of course, the other thing that we need to define is "success". We could come up with a thousand definitions. Is it based on social function, financial success, peer approval, a level of happiness? For the purpose of this book, we will try to simplify things. Let's define success as being a top performer in your field.

So, who are the most successful people? The answer probably won't surprise you. It isn't the people with the highest IQs or the people with the highest levels of technical or academic ability. Many of the most successful people have average IQs and education levels. So if it isn't technical skill, higher education, or intellectual intelligence, what makes people successful?

According to David Caruso, another leader in the field of emotional intelligence, most successful people have learned to "accurately identify emotions, use these emotions to influence how [they] think, understand the underlying causes of these emotions, and manage with emotions by integrating the wisdom of these feelings into [their] thinking." 3 Beyond that, most successful people have learned to understand emotions in others and make true emotional connections. According to Irwin Federman, a partner at US Venture Partners, great leaders know that "people will work harder for someone they like, and they like you in direct proportion to the way you make them feel."

All things being equal, the people who excel are the ones with higher levels of emotional intelligence. Not that technical ability is unimportant. In fact, it is important for success, especially in the construction industry. But technical ability and experience can only take you so far. One construction leader called it "the price of entry", but once that technical knowledge is in place, emotional intelligence is vital for ongoing success. One program participant put it this way, "Relationships and impressions are just as important as bricks and mortar."

The following is a graphical representation of the emotional intelligence and knowledge axes. The highlighted box indicates where most construction managers lie. For the purposes of this book, we will use "construction manager" as a generic term to include anyone who is involved in managing the various parts of the construction process. These managers tend to have medium to high levels of specialized knowledge, but average to low emotional intelligence and even lower interpersonal skills.

HIGH EMOTIONAL INTELLIGENCE	
steady performer	high performers
moderate to high success	high success
may hit career limit	good life/work balance
great relationships	low stress
moderate to high happiness	high happiness
medium to high stress	self development
	great relationships
LOW KNOWLEDGE (education, cognitive learning/tech ability)	HIGH KNOWLEDGE (education, cognitive learning/tech ability)
low performers	technically trained
inability to maintain relationships	PhD's, researchers
inability to maintain jobs	engineers
unhappy	can't deal w/people
high stress	poor relationships
blames others	medium to high stress
LOW EMOTIONAL INTELLIGENCE	

Most construction folks tend to be in the highlighted box.

The technically educated people in the construction industry such as civil engineers and building construction majors receive very little "people skills" training while in school. There are few courses on interpersonal relationships, communication, empathy, or teamwork. I have also investigated the curricula of several MBA programs, and most of those programs do not adequately cover these areas either. It is a fundamental flaw in our education system, especially for technical people. Those who come up through the field under a mentor with good people skills will have a greater tendency to use these skills. But if they came up under one of those "old school" managers, they may be using the old "kick ass and take names" style to their own detriment.

Managers who focus on these non–technical skills and embrace emotional intelligence become better leaders. One program participant said, "Improving my emotional intelligence builds up my self-confidence and optimism. I started to think and act a lot more using emotional intelligence. We have stressful situations in my business unit and this has helped me to take my company through the hard times." These leaders have learned to tap into that very important part of themselves. They have discovered that they can measure and improve these "soft skills", change behaviors, and increase performance. They become more effective both personally and professionally. There are dozens of testimonials documenting improvements in leadership skills and people skills as a result of this work with emotional intelligence. See the appendix for case studies of companies and managers who have enhanced their emotional intelligence, increased their effectiveness, and improved the way they work.

There are several instruments that measure emotional intelligence. One of the best instruments is the Bar-On Emotional Quotient Inventory, or EQ-i®. This evaluation was seventeen years in development, and there are over 1,000,000 evaluations in the database. Reuven Bar-On coined the term "EQ" (Emotional

Quotient) to represent emotional competence as opposed to IQ (Intellectual Quotient), which measures intellectual capacity. The Bar-On EQ-i® is a validated, self-perception instrument that measures five main scales (intrapersonal, interpersonal, stress management, adaptability, and general mood). Within each of these scales, there are individual competencies or subscales. Here are the definitions of each of these competencies:

INTRAPERSONAL:

Self-Regard is the ability to respect and accept oneself as basically good. It is also related to self-confidence.

Emotional Self-Awareness is the ability to recognize one's feelings and share them appropriately with others.

Assertiveness is the ability to express feelings, beliefs and thoughts and defend one's rights in a non-destructive manner.

Independence is the ability to be self directed and self-controlled in one's thinking and actions and to be free from emotional dependency.

Self-Actualization is the ability to realize one's potential, using your talents to the best of your ability, to be generally satisfied with your life.

INTERPERSONAL:

Empathy is the ability to be aware of, to understand, and to appreciate the feelings of others. (Note: This is not to be confused with sympathy, which is feeling sorry for the other person.)

Social Responsibility is the ability to demonstrate oneself as a co-operative, contributing, & constructive member of a larger group.

Interpersonal Relationships is the ability to establish and maintain mutually satisfying relationships.

STRESS MANAGEMENT:

Stress Tolerance is the ability to withstand adverse events and stressful situations without "falling apart" by actively and positively coping with stress.

Impulse Control is the ability to resist or delay an impulse, drive, or temptation to act.

ADAPTABILITY:

Reality Testing is the ability to see the real situation and not be overly optimistic or pessimistic.

Flexibility is the ability to adjust one's emotions, thoughts and behavior to changing situations and conditions.

Problem Solving is the ability to identify and solve problems as well as to generate and implement potentially effective solutions.

GENERAL MOOD:

Optimism is the ability to look at the brighter side of life and to maintain a positive attitude, even in the face of adversity.

Happiness is the ability to feel satisfied with one's life, to enjoy yourself and others, and to have fun.

When this EQ-i® evaluation is taken, the results are compared against a normative group, or a large group of people who have taken the evaluation. The numerical results for each competency fall into a bell curve. Similar to an IQ test, 100 is the mean or average. Scores ranging from 90-110 are considered average or adequate emotional functioning. Scores higher or lower than this range can indicate that the respondent is above or below average. By measuring these fifteen competencies and more importantly, by comparing the relationships among them, we can determine problem areas to target for improvement.

Hundreds of people in the construction industry have taken this evaluation and not one has said that the results were invalid. In fact, almost all of the people to whom we have given feedback have agreed that the evaluation was quite accurate. The validity scales that are built into the evaluation bear this out as they are usually well within the normal range. I believe it is because of the participants' desire to be accurate. They want the results to reflect their behavior. Occasionally, respondents tell us that they think some of their low scores, such as empathy or interpersonal relationship skills, are inaccurate. When this happens, we ask them to show the results to the people who know them well, such as their spouse or close friend or colleague. Each time they have returned and told us that these other people agree with their EQ-i® results indicating that they probably do need to work on those particular skills.

After seeing hundreds of these EQ profiles for construction folks, a definite pattern emerged. Although there were individual differences, every group with whom we worked had virtually the same EQ profile. We have aggregated all of the scores from over three hundred construction managers into a group EQ profile for the construction industry. This group includes fifty different companies from all over the world and a wide cross section of people from various parts of the construction industry including general contractors, subcontractors, vendors, suppliers, construction managers, design firms, and architectural firms. The positions include assistant superintendents, superintendents, assistant project managers, project managers, senior project managers, subcontractor owners and employees, architects, engineers, building construction majors, business unit managers, estimators, sales people, production people, vice presidents, senior vice presidents, business developers, project executives, and a small number of support folks such as accountants, marketing staff, human resource, and information technology people. Although most of the participants were men, there were a few women. (Find the EQ profile on the next page.)

The first thing that stands out is a relatively low score in emotional self-awareness, which is key for good emotional management. Also note the relatively high assertiveness, indepen-

TYPICAL CONSTRUCTION MANAGER EQ PROFILE

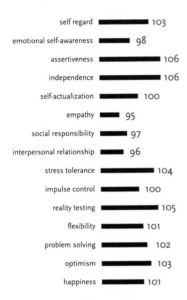

self regard	103
emotional self-awareness	98
assertiveness	106
independence	106
self-actualization	100
empathy	95
social responsibility	97
interpersonal relationship	96
stress tolerance	104
impulse control	100
reality testing	105
flexibility	101
problem solving	102
optimism	103
happiness	101

dence, and self-regard in contrast to low scores on emotional self-awareness and interpersonal skills across the board (low empathy, low social responsibility, and low interpersonal relationship skills). Keep in mind that this is an average profile. Some of the participants scored quite high in interpersonal skills, making the average higher. We have worked with some participants whose interpersonal scores were in the 50s.

This group also tends to have high stress tolerance and low impulse control. This is a chaos profile based on a reactive management style which is inherent in the industry. Most managers go from crisis to crisis. This group scores high in reality testing, which means that they are neither overly optimistic nor pessimistic and usually see things in black and white. In addition, the self-actualization and happiness scores for this group tend to be low. This speaks volumes about the industry today. Many believe that it just isn't as enjoyable as it used to be.

With this typical profile, most construction managers are perceived as aggressive, independent, and capable, but may also come across as people who don't listen, seldom ask for input from others, or won't involve others in the decision making process at all. They are often blunt and undiplomatic, have a hard time delegating, and tend to micromanage. Due to this crisis management style, they usually spend little time developing themselves or mentoring subordinates.

Also note that without the strong interpersonal skills to balance competencies like assertiveness, independence, and self-regard, these strengths can become weaknesses. Someone with high assertiveness can become aggressive, someone with high independence can become a loner who doesn't interact with others, and someone with high self-regard can become arrogant.

Prior to the publication of the first edition of this book, Brian K. Walker of Virginia Polytechnic Institute and State University wrote his Master's Thesis titled Emotional Intelligence Within the A/E/C Industry: A Step Toward Effective Collaboration (May 28, 2003). Mr. Walker's statistical analysis of 104 total participants from seven different companies revealed a typical construction person profile that was almost identical to mine. This data is further evidence of this typical construction manager EQ profile, which seems to be consistent across the industry.

There are other EQ profiles that can indicate performance or behavioral issues. A low score on assertiveness, independence, and self-regard, along with relatively high scores on empathy and social responsibility may indicate a person who has trouble saying no, who gets taken advantage of or walked on. These people may have trouble negotiating and firmly stating their beliefs. This profile is rare in construction managers, but more common for administrative and support positions. It would be very beneficial to know about this profile prior to hiring because this can be problematic for supervisory positions. We've all seen those poor souls who just can't seem to stand up for themselves, but by working on their assertiveness, independence, and self-regard, they can become much more effective.

Low self-actualization along with low happiness and optimism in a forty-plus-year-old may indicate the proverbial mid-life crisis, which could affect productivity at work. Many participants with this profile admit that they are questioning their direction in life and are not satisfied with where they are.

If we can identify this situation early, we can make positive changes before they buy that Harley motorcycle and leave the company on a cross country road trip. This same profile is typical for new parents, especially when the score for social responsibility is also low. You've seen the new father, bleary-eyed and exhausted for the first few months of the baby's life. This certainly affects his productivity at work. Both of these issues can be addressed by working on a clear direction for the employee's life and career and letting them know that this is just a transitory period in their lives.

If you add a low stress tolerance score to this profile, it may indicate burnout. Stress and burnout are huge issues in the industry, and the cost is high in both business and human terms. The statistics on the increase in stress and burnout are alarming. You see these people all of the time in the industry. They are overweight and out of shape, with poor eating habits and dysfunctional lifestyles. They are on the treadmill and see no way off. Accurate evaluation and early identification of stress and burnout along with lifestyle adjustments, diet, exercise, and stress reduction can prevent problems such as absenteeism, low productivity, and stress related illnesses.

High assertiveness, low impulse control, and low flexibility may indicate a problem with anger management or other impulsive behavior. You've seen the guy who storms into the jobsite trailer, yelling and swearing and throwing his hard hat. It's not a pretty sight. By working on these fundamental emotional competencies, managers are better able to control angry outbursts and work toward a fundamental change in behavior. This makes them much more effective in their dealings with project stakeholders.

For the construction industry, there are several advantages to focusing on emotional intelligence as a way to develop people and solve industry problems:

1. Many companies realize the importance of "soft skills" and invest in the training of these skills, but rarely know if the training has been effective. This is a way to measure and improve these skills to produce tangible, fundamental changes in behavior.

2. Emotional intelligence work may answer previously unanswered questions for individuals in your company. Employees may already know that they have difficulty with relationships or anger management problems. They may have been told during their review process that they need to "work on their people skills" or "be nicer to people". The problem is that they may not be able to pinpoint exactly how to do that. But once they take the EQ-i® evaluation and see low scores on empathy or impulse control, they are able to focus on these specific areas to create fundamental behavioral change.

3. Engineers and technically educated or trained people like numbers. As construction people, we are obsessed with them – tolerances, schedule days, budget numbers, manpower, produc-

tivity numbers, etc. Most construction folks are not shy about sharing their scores. They boast of high scores and sheepishly share their low scores (usually in the interpersonal skills) and vow that they will increase them. People in the industry are much more likely to embrace this work because it produces tangible results that can be measured and improved.

Emotional intelligence is imperative for effective performance. If we evaluate our employees' emotional competencies, identify their developmental needs, and help them to work on these areas, they will improve these skills, increase their effectiveness, and eventually contribute more to the bottom line.

2 : *Emotional Intelligence and the Bottom Line*

People work for people, not companies.
A worker's regard for his supervisor will affect his opinion of his
employer. Production is related to attitude, so much so that an
organization which disregards this human equation
will not achieve as much as it could achieve.
—Gerard R. Griffin

WE TALKED IN CHAPTER ONE about the "old school" construction manager. For those of us who have been in the construction industry for a while, we all know who the "old school" construction manager is. He's the one who kicks ass and takes names, the one who gets the job done. He doesn't take crap from anybody, punishes subcontractors, and holds the owner's and the architect's feet to the fire. He doesn't think twice about compromising safety if he thinks it will increase his profit and personal bonus. If the project is a hard bid project, he finds a large percentage of change orders due to errors and omissions in the drawings, specifications, and contracts. He is willing to make others look bad so that his company can look good. It is his philosophy that since the next project will probably be awarded to the low bidder, it is unnecessary to create and maintain good relationships. It is far more important to "win" at all costs.

But the face of construction is changing. The industry is becoming more of a service industry. We are getting away from the notion of delivering a building to an owner and walking away. We are seeing more design-build and negotiated projects, more team approaches beyond mere partnering agreements, more ongoing service contracts, and more repeat business. This "old school" guy is becoming a dinosaur. The new construction manager not only needs high levels of assertiveness, self-regard, and independence, but should also have balance in his emotional makeup. He should be a person who is likeable, with strong empathy, communication, and relationship skills. He should be able to build teams and carry out a project plan with a sense of cooperation, constantly looking for "win-win" outcomes. In short, he needs a higher level of emotional intelligence. One participant put it this way, "It is not what you know, but the way you present things. Leading and motivating is not just pointing and screaming."

Centex Construction is one of the top contractors in the USA. According to John Tarpey, the Division President and CEO for Centex Construction in Washington, DC, there are four basic areas of product delivery for the construction industry-schedule, budget, quality, and relationships. Most contractors are fairly adept at the first three, but it is the last area, the area of relationships, where many contractors fail. Ask yourself what a client remembers a year after a project is complete. Is it that the project was built on time, within a budget with reasonable quality? More likely what will be remembered are the relationships on the project-good or bad.

The chart on the next page is an EQ profile for a forty-seven year old high school educated man who owns a highly successful contracting business (Case Study 4 in the appendix).

His EQ-i® results shown below may explain why he has done so well. This person's total EQ score was close to the upper limits of the average range (112), which suggests that he was well prepared to deal with the usual demands and pressures of everyday life. By studying six of his highest scores, it became quite clear how he became so successful. His intrapersonal strength stems from his positive self-regard (sr=117) and a very high degree of independence (in=127). Moreover, one of his highest scores was in the interpersonal relationship domain (ir=127). These intrapersonal and interpersonal strengths combine with a very high degree of optimism (OP=126), stress tolerance (ST=124), and a down-to-earth, highly developed ability to solve problems (PS=123).

CASE STUDY 4

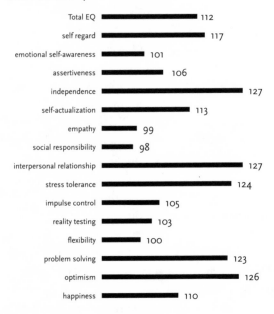

Total EQ	112
self regard	117
emotional self-awareness	101
assertiveness	106
independence	127
self-actualization	113
empathy	99
social responsibility	98
interpersonal relationship	127
stress tolerance	124
impulse control	105
reality testing	103
flexibility	100
problem solving	123
optimism	126
happiness	110

Other people considered him to be a "very good person to work with and for." Interestingly, he received a total IQ score of 102 on an intelligence test that was given toward the end of his last year in high school. An IQ of 102 placed his cognitive intelligence in the middle of the average range; his grades in high school were also average.

Although he had high self-regard and independence similar to the typical construction manager's profile, he has balanced these strong traits with great relationship skills. He has used his emotional intelligence to his advantage which thoroughly prepared him for the paradigm shifts in the construction industry.

Let's take a closer look at some of these shifts:

Old Paradigm	New Paradigm
Large labor pool	Competition for talent
Homogenous labor pool	Multi – cultural labor pool
Manage processes	Manage people
Low bid work	Negotiated work
Short, adversarial relationships	Long, satisfying relationships
Lack of client focus	Focus on client and his needs
Communication lacking	Communication focus
Decrease overhead	Increase performance
Safety a nuisance	Focus on safety
Environmental ignorance	Environmental focus
High stress/burnout	Reduce stress/burnout

This new paradigm requires a different set of skills than the old paradigm. The problem is that the typical emotional intelligence profile for construction folks is in direct contrast to the skills required for this shift. Let's revisit the typical construction industry EQ profile found in Chapter 1.

In an industry where collaboration, good relationships, team work, flexibility, and communication are essential for success, the people who are attracted to this business generally have low emotional self-awareness (lack of understanding of self), high assertiveness (aggressiveness), high independence (not a team player), high self-regard (leaning toward arrogance), low empathy (lack of understanding of others), low social responsibility (they don't work well in groups), and low interpersonal relationship skills. The data is consistent and undeniable. Think about it. Many of the people in the construction industry have this typical profile. No wonder it's such a difficult business!

Emotional intelligence is not some "touchy-feely" approach to management. It's not about group hugs and everyone getting along like robots. As we said before, we are hardwired for emotion, and it is integral to the way we think and interact with people. Understanding others helps us to be more effective. Peter, one of our participants put it this way, "I've learned that being able to understand what is motivating the other parties is essential for achieving your objectives." Another participant called this understanding "a definite competitive advantage". But with this typical EQ profile, understanding others is limited. How many people can you think of in the construction industry with this typical EQ profile? How many employees has your company given up on because of their lack of people skills? Now there is hope for these people. By evaluating and improving their emotional intelligence, they will be able to thrive in this new paradigm.

Most companies are not prepared for these industry shifts, nor do they know how to cope with them. But the key to dealing with these shifts is in addressing the emotional intelligence needs of your employees and your company. In fact, it is critical for your future success. You must give your employees the proper tools, training, and encouragement to survive in this changing climate in the construction industry. You must pay attention to their emotional competencies, evaluate them, identify developmental needs, and provide programs that will enhance their social competence. Without these skills, without the proper emotional tools, managers will fail in this new work environment. Companies who ignore these trends will lose work, lose employees, reduce their margins, and eventually go out of business. But those companies who pay attention to this vital work will hire great people, help them with their emotional development, create lasting client and stakeholder relationships, and thrive in this new marketplace, ultimately adding a great deal to the bottom line.

3 : *Construction Industry Problems*

"You can't win without being completely different.
When everyone else says we're crazy, I say,
'Gee, we must really be onto something.'"
—Larry Ellison, Founder of Oracle

W E ARE NOW GOING TO DELVE into some of the more pressing issues in the industry, focusing on probable causes, potential solutions, and how they affect the bottom line. The root cause of many of the industry problems is due to the typical emotional intelligence profile for construction managers. If we can address these areas and create fundamental change in our people, we can have a profound effect on the entire industry.

SAFETY ISSUES: Anyone who has ever been on a project where there was a serious accident knows that horrible feeling in the pit of your stomach when the radio crackles with the news that someone has been badly injured or killed, and you hear the siren of an ambulance in the distance. No matter how successful the project is, that is the one thing that will always be remembered.

Safety is a huge issue. Not only is there a moral imperative to improve safety, but accidents and other safety issues cost the industry billions of dollars per year in high insurance costs, lawsuits, Occupational Health and Safety Administration (OSHA) fines, and image problems.

We all know that construction is a hazardous occupation. In the United States, during the period from 1980 through 1995, at least 17,000 construction workers died from injuries suffered on the job. Can you imagine what these statistics are worldwide? In the United States, construction lost more workers to death from traumatic injury than any other major industrial sector during this time period. Construction has the third highest rate of death by injury: 15.2 deaths per 100,000 workers. This figure for 2005 dropped to 11 deaths per 100,000 workers, but it is still high. Only mining and agriculture experience higher rates. The leading causes of death among construction workers are falls from elevations, motor vehicle crashes, electrocution, machine accidents, and being struck by falling objects.[4]

What is the problem? Do people want to work unsafely? If you ask them this question, their answer is a resounding "NO!" When you ask top managers if they want their people to work unsafely, they answer, "Of course not!" So what is the problem here? The present system to ensure project safety is a command and control approach where strict safety rules are implemented. If the rules are not followed, the offending employee is reprimanded or fired. This approach has been marginally successful, but because we have only focused on the objective side of safety, we have reached the limit of its success. To achieve the next level, we must tap into the subjective side and use emotional intelligence.

A contractor had five elevator workers that were not working safely. They were not tying off as they should. The superintendent called them into the trailer and had a talk with them. He sent them home and told them to get a letter from their wives saying that it was okay for them to work unsafely. As soon as he had those letters in his hands, they could go back to work. The elevator guys were a little stunned, and sheepishly went home early. The next day, four of the wives visited the project, and the other one called. They told the superintendent that their husbands had a responsibility to their families to come home alive and unhurt each day, and if their husbands were not working safely to please call them, and they would straighten out that situation in very short order. This is a great use of emotional intelligence with regard to safety.

When you think about it, every person on every project has loved ones – a family, a spouse, a partner, a friend, a child, a brother, a sister, a mother, or a father. When you look at safety from this highly personal perspective and make the emotional connections, when you put it in those personal terms, safety becomes much more than rules and regulations. Specifically, social responsibility, interpersonal relationships, and empathy skills are the keys to a safer work environment.

There is a popular video making the rounds these days called "Remember Charlie" (www.charliemorecraft.com) in which Charlie Morecraft tells the story of his horrific accident. Charlie didn't follow safety procedures or wear the correct personal protective equipment. The result was a massive fire at a refinery that could have been avoided. Charlie was burned over 50% of his body and took five years out of his life to heal. The film depicts how his injury and recovery almost destroyed his life, and how it affected his family. His father had a stroke shortly after the accident, he and his wife divorced, and both of his daughters missed having a "daddy" around while they were growing up. He tells of the agony his mother faced each day having to watch him go through the extreme pain of "de-breeding", a procedure in which the dead skin from the burns is removed in large chlorine tubs. Even the most hard-hearted superintendent wipes tears away after seeing this video. With an emotionally intelligent approach, safety is no longer a set of rules to begrudgingly follow. There is a paradigm shift. Charlie gives safety a human side.

Bovis Lend Lease in Atlanta has used this type of program with dramatic results. In the United States, insurance companies assign a modifier based on past safety performance. This modifier is called the EMR (Experience Modification Ratio). This EMR determines what companies will pay for liability insurance.

The more safely a company works, the lower their EMR. Let's use an example: Say you are buying $100,000 worth of liability insurance for a project. If your EMR is 1.0 (an EMR of 1.0 is the industry standard), you will pay $100,000 for that insurance. If your EMR is 1.5, you will pay $150,000 for the same insurance. If your EMR is 0.5, you will pay $50,000 for that insurance. Using an emotionally intelligent approach to safety, Bovis Lend Lease reduced their EMR to 0.34, so they would pay only $34,000 for that insurance. Bovis Lend Lease is not only saving lives and reducing emotional turmoil, but they are saving money and improving their bottom line. Imagine if the entire industry used this approach. The potential cost savings would be staggering, but the potential to decrease human suffering due to death and disability would be even greater.

Let's look at how some other industry issues relate to safety. Communication and teamwork are vital to working safely. Poor communication and ineffective teamwork can contribute to poor safety practices. Controlling stress and burnout can also be a significant factor in preventing accidents. When we are tired or stressed, we have a greater tendency to make mistakes. And mistakes on a construction project can be fatal.

The key to this approach to safety is the emotional intelligence of the people on the projects; therefore the typical construction worker profile must be addressed first. We must increase empathy skills, relationship skills, and social responsibility if these types of programs are to be successful. If we address these core issues, identify them, and take steps to improve them, we can create fundamental change that will help to take safety to a new level. When people actually make emotional connections and care about each other, they look out for each other and work safer naturally. And when people work more safely, companies will save millions by lowering insurance rates, reducing worker's compensation claims, decreasing wrongful death lawsuits, and increasing productivity.

We have developed a safety program called Primal Safety®. This unique program states that everyone has the basic human right to go home alive and free from injuries at the end of the day. But with that right comes the responsibility to watch out for each other, to care for each other enough to point out unsafe situations, and to take the necessary corrective actions.

PRIMAL SAFETY®: A GUT LEVEL APPROACH The costs for not working safely can be monumental both in financial and human terms. Most safety programs are comprised of objective rules and regulations. When it comes to safety, there is a right way and a wrong way to work. Even though there are severe consequences when these rules are broken, workers still may not follow these rules. Why is that? According to philosopher, Ken Wilbur, these objective approaches, as effective as they are, will always hit a limit, a barrier. In order to break through this barrier, you must tap into the subjective side of safety, the primal side, the emotional side. Emotional responses are far more powerful than responses to rules and regulations. Once you tap into these emotional responses to safety, this objective barrier is breached and you will improve the effectiveness of your overall safety program.

Primal Safety® uses the following methodology:

Employees and project teams focus on emotional competencies such as empathy and interpersonal relationship skills. Key team members should take the EQ-i® and develop the areas that are required for a successful program.

Employees and project teams form closer relationships with each other with a deliberate approach to relationship building.

Employees and project teams learn about each other's lives

outside of work. This is done both formally and informally through activities for the workers and their families. Family members and loved ones become part of the safety process.

Employees and project teams develop a greater awareness of safety – not because of rules but because the workers will care enough about each other to keep each other safe.

Primal safety program specifics:

1 The purpose of this program is to enhance the safety program that you already have in place.

2 The project team and any other appropriate parties take the Emotional Quotient Inventory (EQ-i®). This measures their social competence, including areas such as empathy and interpersonal relationships. Without this foundation, typical construction EQ profiles will likely limit the effectiveness of this program. One of the highest competencies measured by the EQ-i® for construction folks is independence. We will emphasize that by working unsafely and being involved in an accident, workers may experience a great loss of independence, something that is very important to them.

3 The basic premise of the Primal Safety® program is that everyone in your company has a moral imperative to implement an effective safety program for all workers, including subcontractors, affording every worker the basic human right to go home each day uninjured to their family and loved ones. This means ZERO TOLERANCE! No accident or unsafe situation, no matter how small or insignificant, is acceptable. This approach is similar to how Rudy Giuliani, the former mayor of New York, cleaned up New York City. It was called the broken window theory. When there was a broken window, it was replaced. When graffiti showed up, it was removed the same day. There was zero tolerance of the smallest of infractions, because if minor infractions were not addressed, it led to larger infractions and more serious crimes.

4 All employees are encouraged to report any accident, potential accident, or unsafe situation, no matter how small. Every report is acted upon. Blame is not assessed, violators are not punished, and reporters are thanked and encouraged. The process is as follows:

a. Analyze why the hazardous situation exists.

b. Correct the situation.

c. Educate the violators as to the proper means and methods in the spirit of learning and improving.

d. Communicate these reports to everyone in order to avoid this situation in the future.

5 As part of the safety orientation, all employees watch a safety video. This video depicts interviews with workers who have been disabled by workplace injuries as well as interviews with their family and friends. The employees learn that these injuries not only rob them of their independence, but also create ripple effects that touch many people. This is a powerful way to make safety a personal issue.

6 All safety activities are tracked and recorded including accidents, avoided accidents, unsafe situations and behaviors, corrective actions, and communications. Everyone has access to this information, which is reinforced at all meetings.

7 There are numerous activities to reinforce these safety concepts. Some ideas:

a. Each morning, the entire project team does five to ten minutes of calisthenics and warm-up exercises. This reinforces the team approach to safety and prevents accidents by getting the blood flowing, warming up joints, and waking the team up mentally. We provide specific instructions to project team leaders on how to conduct this morning session. You may also use this session to highlight a safety issue for the day.

b. Safety milestones are celebrated with jobsite lunches and team activities. These celebrations are also an opportunity to enhance the spirit of the team and create closer relationships among the workers.

c. There are social activities outside of work to encourage the workers to create closer relationships with each other. These may include sports activities, team sports, and other social activities.

d. The toolbox safety meetings not only discuss best safety practices, rules, and regulations, but they address the emotional side of safety as well. We provide specifics on this to the project teams in charge of these meetings.

e. Celebrations of birthdays, anniversaries, births, life milestones, etc are encouraged. These celebrations reinforce the human side and put a face on safety.

8 There are family/social activities that reinforce safety. Some ideas:

a. All of the children of the workers make safety posters encouraging their parents to come home safely to them each day. The posters are laminated and placed throughout the project. A safety coloring book for all of the workers' children teaches them about how their parent stays safe while on the job.

b. There are family days so that family members can visit the workplace and see demonstrations of the safety equipment that keeps their loved ones safe.

c. There are family social days such as picnics and parties. Every employee has someone who cares about his or her safety. Employees are not numbers. They are sons, daughters, fathers, mothers, brothers, and sisters.

d. Workers are encouraged to take their safety equipment home and show their families how this equipment protects them from getting hurt on the job.

e. Families are involved in the safety process. If there is a habitual violator, the family can be called in to help motivate that worker. This type of intervention has the potential to save lives.

THE FUTURE OF SAFETY: Where do you go after you reach zero accidents?

For a moment, look to the future and see a vision where the construction industry is not only a safe industry, but actually becomes restorative. Imagine people working in this industry for years and retiring not only free from disabilities, but healthy and full of vigor. That is the next step in this process. Some say it is impossible to achieve. Some use the excuse that "this is a dangerous industry". Although there is no doubt that the work is tough and dangerous, we firmly believe that we can reach that level of health and safety through this emotionally intelligent approach.

STRESS, BURNOUT AND LIFE BALANCE ISSUES: The construction industry has always been stressful, but according to a recent global study compiled by the International Metal Worker's Federation, stress and burnout in the construction industry are on the rise around the world. Our workers are being asked to do more with less. The physical and mental demands are tremendous. Many employees are working 60, 80, even 100-hour weeks, sometimes for extended periods of time.

Take a look at some of the people who have been in the industry a while. Many of them look older than they are, and appear beaten down and worn out. Frequently, these workers develop stress related illnesses such as heart disease, high blood pressure, and diabetes. A surprising number depend on nicotine and caffeine in the morning to get started and alcohol at night to calm down. Many use both prescription and over-the-counter medications to control the symptoms of stress such as headaches, stomach problems, allergies, pain, fatigue, difficulty sleeping, and irritability. When managing projects, I used to visit the shiny white first aid box with the big blue cross on the door a couple of times a day. I would reach in and remove the small, individual packets of sweet relief, popping aspirin for my daily stress headaches. After wolfing down my lunch consisting of a chili dog and French fries from the roach coach (the endearing term for the break truck), I would reach for a few antacids as a preemptive strike on my afternoon stomach problems. It was much easier to pop pills rather than address the underlying stressors, which were the cause of many of these symptoms.

Many companies are beginning to wake up to this reality and address this issue. Using emotional intelligence, we can measure stress and burnout by measuring such traits as stress tolerance, self-actualization, happiness, and optimism. That way, we can determine if stress and burnout are problems and deal with them before they manifest themselves in the form of sickness, low productivity, absenteeism, and chronic disease.

According to Daniel Goleman, a leader in the emotional intelligence field, stress can be a killer, especially for those who have heart disease, the number one killer in this country. "Distressing feelings – sadness, frustration, anger, tension, intense anxiety – double the risk that someone with heart disease may experience a dangerous decrease in blood flow to the heart within hours of having these feelings. Such a decrease can trigger a heart attack."[5]

There is mounting evidence of this link between stress and general health. According to the World Health Organization, 80–90% of illnesses are either caused by or made worse by stress.

The United States is the only industrialized nation on earth without a paid leave law. It's no coincidence that we are also the most stressed nation on earth. In the United States, we simply don't have enough downtime. Compared to other countries, our holidays and vacation days are ridiculously low. Most workers in other countries have a minimum of five weeks vacation and some have as many as nine. Even the Chinese have a law requiring employers to give their employees a minimum of three weeks of paid vacation.

This may sound ludicrous to all of us hardworking, take-no-prisoners Americans. I've known several construction folks who wear their lack of vacation as a badge of honor. They boast, "I haven't had a vacation in ten years!" But what is the cost? We are becoming a nation of stressed-out people with autoimmune maladies, hypertension, diabetes, cancer, and heart disease. In the United States, we spend over $222 billion per year on legal drugs. Per capita spending on healthcare per year, which is $5,711 per person, is the highest in the world.[6] Many of these drugs are prescribed to alleviate the symptoms of stress related illnesses. Recent studies also indicate that there may be a link between stress and obesity, an emerging health issue in the United States. We must change the way we think about our time off or face these dire health consequences.

Europeans we interviewed said that they need at least three weeks' vacation because during the first and last weeks, they are still thinking about work. With three or more weeks of vacation, they are able to have at least one week of total decompression. We just can't get there with a mere two weeks per year. We usually take those two weeks in installments of three and four day weekends. It just isn't enough. With these diminished vacation times, we very rarely reach a true state of decompression, especially when we take our phones and check our emails each day. According to a study in the book, Work to Live: The Guide for Getting a Life, a yearly vacation was found to reduce the risk of heart attack by 30% in men and 50% in women.[7]

What if companies started offering more vacation time, more flextime, and more ways for their employees to recover? The costs would be minimal compared with the results. Most people we interviewed said they would take a substantial cut in pay to be able to have more time off. Just by investing a little bit into their people, companies would have happier, less stressed, more loyal, more productive employees.

Vacation is certainly one way to help deal with stress. But the day-to-day stress issues should be aggressively confronted by teaching managers to recognize symptoms of stress in their bodies, reduce these stressors, and build in recovery activities for renewal. This focus on stress reduction and recovery times allows them to have better performance mentally and physically. Another important issue is teaching managers how to create better life balance. One participant told us, "I have increased the balance in life, which has increased my efficiency at work."

One very effective way to renew the body is by doing yoga and meditation. During our courses, managers are taught these basic techniques as a way to reduce stress and create better focus. This work with yoga and meditation is outside the comfort zones of most construction folks. I remember an incident from the first day of a management development program for a large, international contractor. It was very early in the morning, and we were starting with basic yoga and meditation. The room was empty except for some yoga mats. There was meditative music playing. I watched as these tough construction guys entered, walked back out to make sure it was the right room, then slowly came back in and sat down on their mats.

The thing that surprises me most about introducing yoga and meditation to the construction industry is that almost half of the participants who have been exposed to yoga and meditation during our courses have continued these practices afterwards. Even though some are reluctant to admit that they are actually doing yoga, they continue to practice it because of the tremendous benefits. Claus, a business unit president from Denmark said to me, "I think this yoga stuff is crap, but that deep breathing really helps me to reduce my stress."

Mariann, a controller from Sweden, was having trouble sleeping and sent me the following via email: "My job situation is extremely hectic again, and I have had some problems sleeping. Last night, however, I was able to calm down and relax using your meditation CD." Tom, a project manager from the United States put it this way, "Without question, the most helpful skill which I have implemented from my emotional intelligence training is how to better handle and reduce stress. By better controlling stress, I have seen positive results both at work and in my private life."

There is another benefit to yoga and meditation besides stress reduction. It actually enhances the emotional intelligence learning process. Because we are essentially rewiring the brain, creating new neural pathways, the yoga and mediation techniques help to create these new highways in the brain and speed up the behavioral shifts. We also use visualization techniques to improve emotional competencies. Participants will visualize situations and outcomes that reinforce the behaviors that they want to achieve.

The more we study the brain, the more we see the connection between the mind and body. When we reduce stress, we reduce cortisol, a hormone that is secreted during the "fight or flight" response. Cortisol shuts down the thinking brain because when you are being chased by a tiger, it is not in your best interest to over-analyze the situation. Without this hormone rush, we are able to think more clearly and solve problems more readily. We are able to be in a concept called "flow", where body and mind are in harmony with each other and both work as efficiently as possible. This results in fewer sick days and more stamina. Study after study confirms what we already know to be true. If we are sharp mentally, we function better physically and vice versa. Reducing stress through meditation has also been shown to increase the immune response and improve the body's healing process.

Yoga and meditation certainly aren't for everyone, but we encourage participants to find "their" yoga. For some it is a sport such as golf, hunting, fishing, sailing, or some kind of hobby or recreational pursuit. It may be music or exercise or spending time with their family. On one project we had laugh time. Every day from 3:00 to 3:15, we gathered in the trailer to laugh. Sometimes we told jokes. Sometimes we just laughed. It became this spontaneous thing that relieved tension and helped us to be more productive. This message of laughter has caught on in a big way. Laugh clubs are being formed all over the world. In fact, Glaxo and Volvo have organized laugh clubs in their organizations because of the positive benefits. No matter what you decide to do, the important thing is building in that reflection time and downtime each day where work is no longer the focus.

Companies are starting to realize the importance of addressing these health issues for their workers not only to make them more productive, but also to curb high healthcare costs. In an article titled, "Wellness Program Cures Rising Health Care Costs"[8], Cianbro Corporation, a large heavy civil and industrial contractor, addressed rising healthcare costs head-on. In 2001, they paid $11.5 million in healthcare costs, but these costs were projected to reach $20 million by 2004. So, in 2001, they started a voluntary wellness program for their employees. They reduced the percentage of smokers from 46% to 20%. 34% of their employees are exercising on a regular basis, and there has been a 20% reduction in hypertension and a 25% reduction in high cholesterol. Since 2001, instead of almost doubling, their healthcare costs have remained flat. They conservatively estimate that they get a $3.50 return per every dollar they invest in the wellness program, and this money goes straight to the bottom line.

This high level of stress and burnout relates to other problem areas. Stress decreases productivity. Pete, a project manager sent me the following: "One example of the benefit [of stress management] for me is that I used to take painkillers regularly for frequent stress–related headaches. Now I have learned to deal with the root cause of the headaches, and I rarely take painkillers unless I am really ill." By addressing the underlying cause of these headaches, Pete is now less stressed and more productive. Burnout also contributes to high turnover rates. Employees may leave their jobs in order to reduce their stress. Stressed workers also tend to make more mistakes, which can negatively affect safety, increase costs, and reduce the bottom line.

COACHING ALPHA MALES: It always begins with a phone call. A top manager will call me and say, "I've got this guy. He's a great guy, very competent and knowledgeable. But he's pissing everybody off. Can you help him?" I've had more than a dozen of these calls about these alpha males. The industry is filled with them. They are strong, tough, highly motivated leaders who have a commanding presence and an aggressive style. These alpha males think they can do anything. My father, an alpha male in his younger days, tells a story of when he was a young carpenter. The layout engineer quit on a Friday afternoon and the superintendent asked my father if he could lay out the building. My father assured him that he could, then went home Friday to try and figure out how to lay out a building. He called a friend of his who brought over a transit and taught him how to use it over the weekend. In the end, he laid out the building without any difficulty.

These alpha males are extremely effective in certain areas, but according to an article titled "Coaching the Alpha Male" by Kate Ludeman and Eddie Erlandson, if these alpha males develop their interpersonal skills, they are even more effective. According to Ludeman and Erlanson, "Because [Alpha Males] believe that paying attention to feelings, even their own, detracts from getting the job done, they're surprisingly oblivious to the effect they have on others. They're judgmental of colleagues who can't control their emotions, yet often fail to notice how they vent their own anger and frustration. Or they dismiss their outbursts, arguing that the same rules shouldn't apply to the top dog."[9]

They further state "the best way to capture the alpha male's attention is with data-copious, credible, consistent data." Our goal is to provide undeniable proof that his behavior (to which he is much attached) doesn't work nearly as well as he thinks it does." We use the Bar-On EQ-i®, which gives the alpha male a graphical representation of his social functioning. If he is skeptical about the instrument, we can utilize the 360 EQ-i®, where the employees rate their own EQ while their subordinates, peers, supervisors, clients, family, and friends rate them as well. We do this to provide the "copious, credible, consistent data" that gets through to them. Once the alpha male sees this data, we have a better chance of convincing him that we can make him even more effective by improving his interpersonal skills. One participant put it this way, "Becoming aware of your own and other people's emotions makes you a powerful person."

If alpha males don't keep their assertiveness and self regard in check, they can limit a company's financial success. As Daniel Goleman states, "A cranky and ruthless boss creates a toxic organization filled with negative underachievers who ignore opportunities; an inspirational, inclusive leader spawns acolytes for whom any challenge is surmountable. The final link in the chain is performance: profit or loss."[10]

There was an alpha male named Ragnar in one of the programs I facilitated. During one of the moments where we share our thoughts about the program in front of the group, he said, "When I first started this program, I thought all of you were stupid. But the longer I am around you, the smarter you become." He was saying in his alpha male way that he was becoming smarter and more in tune with his emotional side. At the end of the program he declared, "[The program] has, against all my own odds, made me human."

In the book, Joe Torre's *Ground Rules for Winners*, Joe Torre, the manager for the New York Yankees, discusses how he deals with the large egos in Major League Baseball. He says it's not about a command and control attitude, but about knowing and caring for these world-class athletes in a personal way. If they know that you care about them and are looking out for them, they perform well. In his words, "To develop this level of knowledge about your team players, you need some insight into their personal and emotional qualities."[11]

One of my favorite alpha male stories involves a superintendent in his mid-forties who was reluctant to accept the validity of this work. Although he scored low on empathy and interpersonal relationships, he didn't see it as a problem. During our first session, he told me that he didn't really see a need to work on any of these competencies. He insisted that his job performance was excellent. And it was. I explained to him that I wasn't here to fix him because he wasn't broken. My job was to try and find ways to make him more effective. I asked him to share his EQ-i® evaluation with people he trusted, and ask them if they thought he could benefit by embracing this work.

The more he thought about it, the more he was convinced that this would help his life and his career. So he made up his mind to give this emotional intelligence idea a try. Once he understood the concepts, he became highly committed to his personal development. He read dozens of books, applied the learning each day, and brought his entire project team in on the process of helping him to improve. After about six months, during one of our follow-up discussions, I asked him if others had noticed any behavioral shifts in him. He asked his superiors to let me know if they had noticed any changes. His supervisor sent me the following email. I have changed the participant's name to maintain anonymity: "Bill has worked with me since 1998, and the recent changes are nothing less than remarkable. Since starting with our company, his ability and potential were obvious, but Bill resisted the necessary behavioral changes required to realize his potential. In the past, Bill struggled to maintain working relationships with individuals that did not display his level of commitment and was not understanding of those with lesser abilities. This created a lot of friction over the years as Bill's work ethic, determination, and ability are not easily matched. He is starting a new project as lead superintendent, and I think this will be Bill's opportunity to prove to all that he is truly one of our very best." Another superior added "I completely agree. Bill has really turned it around. I think he is a future star."

For the many alpha males in the construction industry, this emotional intelligence work can make them even more effective by tempering their dominant attitudes and behaviors with great interpersonal skills and impulse control. They will likely be resistant at first, as most construction managers and alpha males are, but once they see the benefits and become aware of the errors associated with their present leadership style, they doggedly pursue this work and become better leaders. They will also be able to more effectively deal with all of the project stakeholders.

POOR INDUSTRY IMAGE: As most of you well know, the

construction industry has a poor image. After performing my own informal survey asking many people about their experiences with contractors, their responses were invariably negative. Most contractors are viewed as unethical, untrustworthy, and difficult to deal with. I remember watching one of those Naked Gun spoof movies. They lampooned just about everyone from law enforcement officials to politicians. When the villain was asked how he could do something so vicious, he replied, "It was easy my dear, don't forget I spent two years as a building contractor."

The Jobs Rated Almanac by Les Krantz ranks the top 250 jobs each year based on several factors of desirability such as pay, benefits, special perks, safety and security, stress risks, environmental conditions, physical demands, career outlook, and travel opportunities. Year after year, construction industry jobs are rated at the very bottom. In 2005, the highest construction related job was ranked at 210. Of the bottom forty jobs, twelve were in the construction industry.[12]

Industry professionals have tried to address this image issue with little success. In the United States, The National Construction Image Steering Committee created the "Industry Image Initiative" to examine these image problems and explore potential solutions, but their progress has been slow. There was an editorial in the May 10, 2004 issue of Engineering News Record titled, "Industry Image Initiative May Be Dying". The editorial states that very little progress has been made to improve the industry image. In fact, it seems to be getting worse.

From the age of fifteen, I worked every summer on various construction projects as a laborer, carpenter's helper, and layout engineer. I loved the work, but I didn't care for some of the people with whom I had to work. They were tough and aggressive. There was one foreman in particular who was downright scary to me. I was afraid to ask about anything for fear that I might appear stupid, and I never wanted to make a mistake. Think of the consequences of this attitude with regard to safety. I remember a time when I stepped on a nail, but was so afraid to tell him, that I went home with a hole in my foot and a blood soaked sock.

Back when I was working summers, the business was tough. Developing a thick skin was a must for survival. There was very little training or orientation. The attitude was, "Throw them in the deep end. If they can't figure it out, we don't want them here." It was like some arcane fraternity, and the initiation process was difficult. These construction people with specialized knowledge would send me after non-existent "board stretchers" and "sky hooks". One time, my boss sent me to fetch a "come-a-long". Well, I had no idea what a "come-a-long" was, but I wasn't about to tell him that. I went to the tool shed and tried to find something that looked like a "come-a-long". Somewhere in the back of my mind, I thought that this was another wild goose chase similar to the "board stretcher" I tried to find the previous week. I was certain that when I returned, everyone would laugh at me. Despite these fears, I pressed on and chose something. By some miraculous twist of fate, I chose the right thing. Now, when I look back at these experiences, I think to myself, "What a screwy business, where you are so afraid of being the butt of a joke that you won't ask when you don't know something."

One other incident sticks in my mind concerning the attitude of the people in the business back then. I was an engineering student at the Georgia Institute of Technology and was working during the summer of 1979 as a layout engineer. We had purchased a Leibherr tower crane, and they sent a German engineer to help with the assembly and setup. We had poured a test weight with hooks embedded in the concrete for the crane to lift. The engineer asked me to determine the weight of the block. I pulled out my trusty handheld calculator along with my handy book that told me the weight per volume for concrete. I punched in the calculation and proudly wrote the result on the top of the concrete block.

Since I fancied myself to be an engineer, I wanted to be really accurate and precise so I carried the number out to six decimal places. When the engineer saw it, he called everyone around and said, "Hey everybody. Look here. Look what the college boy did. He figured up the weight of this piece of concrete." He took out a large Magik Marker, brushed off some of the stray aggregate and dust from the top of the block and marked through all of the numbers after the decimal. "Hey, stupid college boy, when you're dealing with thousands of pounds, you don't need so many decimal places. Or didn't they teach you that in school?" He then brushed more of the dust off, laughed, and said, "That dust I brushed off just changed your number."

Certainly this attitude has improved over the years, but there is still some work to do. It's no wonder that the numbers of young people coming into the industry are dwindling, especially in the trades. Because of these dwindling numbers, we have come to rely on immigrants to fill these positions. Without this influx of immigrants, we would not have the work force to build projects.

There are several factors that contribute to these dwindling numbers. Other industries usually have comparable pay and better benefits such as health insurance, paid vacations, sick days, and retirement programs. Other industries are not as dependent on weather and temperature as the construction industry. If there is a stretch of bad weather, some construction workers are simply not paid. The construction industry has made few adjustments to address these changes in the job market.

There is also a shift in demographics. Baby boomers are beginning to reach retirement age, and there are smaller numbers of generation X and generation Y to replace them.[13] All industries will be competing for this shrinking talent pool. Generation X and generation Y are motivated by a different set of values than the baby boomers. They want to be independent, but also feel like they are part of a family, part of a team. They want to be mentored, coached, and nurtured. They want to make a difference. They are also looking for more balance between work and family. Some companies today may find it difficult to provide this type of atmosphere in the workplace.

There are very few women in this male dominated industry, and the women who are in the industry are mostly in sales and office positions (56%).[14] Those in management positions (23%) have to walk a fine line between assertiveness and compliance. If a woman is too assertive, she is labeled a "bitch". If she is too compliant, she gets little respect. Women will make up 50% of the overall future workforce, and all industries will be competing for them. It would be wise to think about how companies can entice women to enter the construction industry. But if these attitudes don't change, we will lose these capable women to other industries. If we lose the potential talent of women, generation X, and generation Y, we could be driving away the future. An article in the October 30, 2000 Engineering News Record predicted that the construction industry would need to attract more women and minorities in order to grow. This prediction has come to pass and is even truer today.

These demographic and economic issues will be difficult to overcome, but there is one issue that contributes to this industry image problem that we can control. It is the attitudes of the people in the industry. What it boils down to is leadership. We have many managers in the industry, but few leaders. If we deal with this general lack of leadership and focus on leadership qualities like great interpersonal skills, we can greatly improve the industry image. These leaders must learn how to encourage workers and find what they are passionate about. We must teach our leaders to communicate well, to listen and truly care about the people who work for them. This will go a long way toward fixing this poor image while sending the message that this is an industry where you will be respected and encouraged to thrive. If we can find ways to improve this industry image, we will tap into this future workforce, improving clients' trust, working relations, and the way we do business. This will have a direct, positive effect on our bottom line.

POOR CUSTOMER SERVICE: Ask most owners. The perceived level of customer service in the industry is quite low. Not long ago, the Vice President of a top five US contractor said to me, "I think the problem is that we just don't have enough empathy to understand and address the needs of our clients." Given the typical profile for most construction managers, this statement is undeniably true. As a group, most of these managers have low empathy skills, which can prevent them from giving great customer service. If this fundamental lack of empathy is addressed, along with other interpersonal relationship skills, customer service can be significantly improved. One program participant put it this way, "My interpersonal interactions with customers, colleagues, and subordinates have improved by being able to establish a deeper communication."

I had a participant, I'll call him John, a quality control person who was having some difficulty dealing with the representatives from the Corps of Engineers, who have a reputation for being very demanding clients. John scored very high in assertiveness and low in interpersonal relationships and impulse control. He told me that he really didn't like these Corps guys, and he tried to prove them wrong and punish them for their mistakes every chance he got. Most of the time, he just reacted to situations and relished the idea of making them look like fools. I asked him how that was working for him. He said that he felt like he was winning battles, but losing the war.

I had to find something that would work for John, something that would enable him to give the Corps better customer service. As it turns out, John was a devout Catholic. I asked him to picture the Corps representatives with "EGR" stamped on their foreheads. He asked me what "EGR" stood for. I told him, "Extra Grace Required". I pointed out that this was his chance to give them a gift they may not even deserve. He really liked this idea of applying his religious beliefs and implemented it with great results. As he put it, "When faced with a conflict or difference of opinion, I've been very conscientious of letting others speak their minds while concentrating on their positions and feelings. This approach has produced positive outcomes, and I feel that by continuing to use this approach in difficult situations, I will improve and become more successful in resolving conflicts."

His relationship with the Corps improved and enabled him to more easily close out the project.

I would like to share a personal example of poor customer service. I was having a very difficult time with a representative from a company who was creating my website. She was an extremely poor communicator. Sometimes, I thought that we were speaking two different languages. She didn't seem to listen or speak in a way that we both understood. She was very difficult to get along with and didn't understand my needs or try to fulfill them. In order to understand what my company did, she took the EQ-i®. Find her results on the next page.

You can see from her profile why she was so poor at customer service. Her interpersonal skills were extremely low, coupled with relatively high independence, which means she probably would rather keep to herself than deal with anyone, especially someone with problems. She also had very low reality testing, which means

self regard 72
emotional self-awareness 67
assertiveness 62
independence 99
self-actualization 55
empathy 55
social responsibility 66
interpersonal relationship 75
stress tolerance 79
impulse control 95
reality testing 55
flexibility 67
problem solving 69
optimism 87
happiness 79

she likely couldn't understand my situation or the nature of my problems. These traits, along with low flexibility and problem solving, were a recipe for customer service disaster.

Although I could not divulge this person's EQ profile, I talked to the president of this company about this employee's poor customer service. I asked him if he would be interested in a development program using emotional intelligence, coupled with learning modules on communication and customer service training. He declined the offer. I finally had to end the business relationship. How many customers is your company losing because of your employees' poor people skills?

It may not be enough to take your employees through "customer service" training. Given the typical construction managers' profiles, an eight-hour lecture stating a list of things to do to provide great customer service may not be effective since their poor interpersonal skills would prevent them from applying this information in a meaningful way.

Companies must pay attention. Poor customer service due to a lack of people skills may be deteriorating client relationships while you are reading this book. If you address these fundamental emotional competencies now, you can improve your customer service. And improved customer relations mean satisfied clients, referrals, and repeat business, which has a direct impact on your bottom line.

LACK OF TEAMWORK AND TRUST: Does anyone else find it odd that the entire construction industry, to a large extent, is based on mistrust? One survey said that there were only two occupations with a lower level of trust than contractors: television evangelists and used car dealers. We work in an industry where the owner doesn't trust the architect or the contractor, so the work is competitively bid and perhaps a construction manager is hired just to keep an eye on things. The contractor doesn't trust the subcontractors, so again everything is competitively bid. When you think about it, even the term "subcontractor" seems hierarchical and demeaning and doesn't suggest a sense of cooperation. The owner and architect don't trust the contractor, so they are constantly asking for verifications of pricing and methodologies. The contractor doesn't trust the architect or the owner, so he documents everything that is said and done to prepare for claims and litigation. When a problem is encountered, the process, from writing requests for information (RFIs) to processing a change order, is filled with negotiations, conflicts, and arguments. One owner referred to RFIs as Requests for Income. The whole process is adversarial.

Imagine if everyone in the business increased their emotional intelligence, focusing on interpersonal skills, empathy, and social responsibility. When a project was begun, true teams would be created based on mutual trust. When a request for information was written, there would be enough trust so that the problem would be identified and corrected, and the contractor would be paid a fair price for the work without all of the back and forth arguments. They would, in turn, pay the subcontractors their fair share. When I was a project manager, I suggested that we start calling our subcontractors "co-contractors", but my suggestion was met with blank stares or laughter. In Europe, they call these companies "entrepreneurs". It is much more conducive to creating a sense of team.

Think of the time and money spent on cover-your-ass documentation, disagreements, and negotiations on a project. If we could reduce this non-productive workload by creating true teams, imagine how teamwork and productivity would skyrocket. Everyone in the industry would benefit from such a shift, and everyone, including owners, architects, designers, contractors, and subcontractors would be able to add to their bottom line.

Take a look at the following project where lack of teamwork and trust slowed the job progress to the point where they called us for help. This was a $400 million tri-venture hospital project in California. The three contractors were at each other's throats. There was a total lack of trust, gossip was running rampant, and there were several personality conflicts. Teamwork was virtually non-existent. Analyzing the situation using a systems thinking approach, we found what is known as a reinforcing loop. The lack of communication and information sharing caused team members to make assumptions, which were not always accurate. This misinformation led to a lack of trust, which caused the team members to be even more guarded with their communication and information sharing. This resulted in more mistrust, followed by even less information sharing and communication. The cycle continued to reinforce itself until they finally called us. We call this reinforcing loop the downward spiral to hell.

I had a dream the night before this intervention where a fist fight broke out among all of the stakeholders. It looked like one of those bar room brawls in the movies. This was not comforting, but I pressed on. We first did an evaluation of the project team using the EQ-i®. That gave us some clues as to why they were behaving the way they were. Most had the typical construction manager's profile, which was exacerbating the conflicts. We also performed interviews with the managers from the three companies. They were using words like "always" and "never" in their descriptions of situations and people on the project. This was an indication that they were definitely caught in this downward spiral. Using this information, we created a learning program targeting relationships, communication, vision, and team building. By focusing on the people issues, we were able to re-establish the team atmosphere and increase their productivity and effectiveness. One of the project leaders, Tracy MacDonald, a Project Director for McCarthy Construction, credited the intervention with saving the project.

Lack of teamwork can have even more dire consequences. For example, an editorial in the February 21, 2005 Engineering News Record titled "Paris Accident Shows the Need for More Team Building", points out the need for cooperation in the industry. The lack of teamwork may have contributed to the partial collapse of a 640-meter long concourse at Paris Charles de Gaulle airport, which killed four people. The editorial states that, "The Paris collapse shows the need for all parties in the project delivery process to shake off the adversarial pressures and work more tightly as a team."

Perhaps all that project teams need is a larger context. They tend to see thousands of small tasks and very rarely get to see the big picture. I was doing a training session for McCarthy Construction, and we were trying to hone in on which elements contributed to good projects and which ones contributed to bad projects. One of the stories they told was very powerful. They had won the bid to build a cancer research facility for a hospital. Instead of the usual teambuilding and partnering session, the hospital brought in a cancer researcher for the initial meeting.

He told the project team and all of the stakeholders that one in three of them would develop cancer in their lifetime. This facility would be researching cures and preventive measures to reduce the number of deaths from cancer. He impressed upon them that they were building something that may some day save their life or the life of a loved one. What a powerful, emotionally intelligent approach to the creation of a common purpose and a true sense of team!

Even if you aren't building a cancer center, every structure has a purpose, whether that is creating homes for families, schools for learning, buildings for businesses to keep our economy moving, sports and entertainment venues for our pleasure, or infrastructure to help us travel from place to place. I think we have all forgotten what a complex miracle construction is. Putting a building together is one of the most complicated processes you will ever encounter. On your next project, try tapping into that higher sense of purpose and accomplishment in order to create a true sense of team.

These high performing teams are rare, but profound when they come together. Real teams need to have mutual accountability, but with the present project delivery methods that focus on shedding risk, this is impossible. Taking this concept to a higher level, what do you suppose makes a high performing team? One of the requirements is for every team member to care about the other team members and their personal goals, growth, and development. Again, we are tapping into that emotional side of teamwork, where the members create good relationships and have the empathy skills to understand the other team members' goals and aspirations. In short, they create great relationships with each other. One of our participants put it this way, "I think relationships are very important in the construction business. Good relationships with clients mean repeat business, and good relationships with subcontractors mean successful projects." If you pay attention to this emotionally intelligent, relationship focused approach to teambuilding, you will create phenomenal, high performing teams whose successful projects will add more to the company's bottom line.

POOR QUALITY & LOW PRODUCTIVITY: How many times does work-in-place have to be removed because of other work that has been installed out of sequence? How many times does the communication break down and cause something to be delivered late or installed incorrectly? How many times do we improperly handle the architect's and the owner's expectations only to be ambushed during closeout and forced into reworking the finishes? The Construction Industry Institute's research estimates that re-work costs on average 3% of total construction costs. This is money that is being robbed from your bottom line.

During the Total Quality Management revolution and the six sigma sojourns of the 80s and 90s, manufacturers vastly increased their productivity and decreased their defect rates. Unfortunately, the construction industry was virtually bypassed by that whole revolution. Productivity on most projects, even well managed projects, has been far lower than most manufacturers. In a recent productivity survey by FMI, a leading construction industry consultant, "53% of the respondents said that productivity had remained the same, decreased slightly or decreased substantially over the past five years."[15] Low quality is also an issue on most projects because productivity and quality go hand in hand.

One could argue that it is easier to control these factors in a manufacturing setting where there are repetitious work processes. This is undeniably true. But one can also argue that by exploring new, innovative methods, productivity and quality on construction projects can be dramatically increased. There are many tools out there that are supposed to improve quality and productivity: web based information sharing tools, computer aided design systems, personal and handheld computers, digital cameras, lasers, automated transits, and project management and accounting software. And they do improve productivity to some extent. But how do we make that Quantum leap to achieve the same high quality and productivity numbers as manufacturers? By improving the project stakeholders' emotional intelligence, we can improve these areas dramatically. Think about it. Most productivity problems on construction projects are caused by poor communication and poor relationships. Many quality control issues are due to poor communication and preparation and have little to do with expertise. High quality has more to do with motivating the workers to perform the work properly and managing the expectations of the owner and architect. These are directly tied to the social competence of your project team.

Consider this apartment project where the mechanical, electrical, plumbing, and fire protection subcontractors had very poor working relationships. The project had a densely packed hallway, (is there any other kind?), in which the sprinkler contractor had to install his work prior to the ductwork, or his access would be cut off. The sprinkler contractor was behind and had not installed his piping. The duct man installed his ductwork anyway, knowing that the sprinkler man would have to pay him to take the duct down and reinstall it. When the superintendent asked the duct man why he did it, he replied, "I got mine in per the schedule." The superintendent pressed him further. "Didn't you notice that the sprinkler man hadn't installed his work?" His reply was, "F#@! him! I've got a schedule to keep. If I had been late, you would have jumped all over my ass." You can see several problems with this exchange. There was general lack of trust and communication among all of the stakeholders on the project, from the general contractor to the subcontractors. It caused much re-work, decreased quality and productivity, and ate into everyone's project fee.

Emotional intelligence can be used to improve productivity and the quality of the final product. It occurred on a housing project for the 1996 Olympic village, which was being built for the state of Georgia (Georgia State Financing and Investment Commission or GSFIC). At that time, the GSFIC's contracts were difficult and their closeout procedures extremely demanding. Many of their projects took over a year after the certificate of occupancy to close out and receive final payment. The project team had taken the time to do a lot of teambuilding and cultivated great relationships among the mechanical, electrical, plumbing, and fire protection subcontractors. They had a similar situation, a packed hallway in which the sprinkler man needed to install his work prior to the duct. The schedule was accelerated due to some weather related delays, but the sprinkler contractor was not aware of this change. The duct man had a great relationship with the foreman for the sprinkler company, and they often went out after work for a beer. Instead of installing his ductwork ahead of the sprinkler contractor, the duct man notified the sprinkler guy, and they worked out a way to install their work per the schedule, saving re-work and time. This great teamwork contributed to a highly successful project for all of these stakeholders.

In the end, the project was completed ahead of schedule despite seventeen straight days of rain during the foundation work and a damaging fire half way through the project. The key to the success of this project was relationships. Great relationships contributed to great productivity despite many setbacks.

Expectations of the GSFIC and the architect were managed so that everyone knew what to expect at the end of the project with regard to levels of quality. This resulted in a quick closeout. In fact, we closed the project out within 30 days, which was extremely rare for GSFIC projects.

Probably one of the biggest time wasters in the industry is meetings. Why do we have meetings? Think about the topics that are covered at most meetings. Do you focus on positive, productive issues such as teambuilding, vision, relationships, celebrations of milestones, celebrations of project goals, and other human aspects of the project? Or do you focus more on the crises and problems such as conflicts between contractors, owner and architect problems, non-performance issues, poor communication, relationship issues, and cover-your-ass posturing? If the majority of your meetings are taken up with the latter, you may want to take a different approach. If you work to improve the people side of your project that promotes great relationships and positive communication, you will spend less time on the problems. Stephen Covey, author of The 7 Habits of Highly Effective People, would call the focus on the crises a Quadrant I approach, or activities that are important and urgent. The focus on productive issues is a Quadrant II approach. These activities are important, but not urgent. If more time is spent in Quadrant II, less time will be spent in Quadrant I. This means higher productivity and more money to the bottom line.

Stress and burnout can negatively affect productivity. When we are tired and stressed, we aren't nearly as productive. When we work past our effective limits, productivity decreases. Some studies effectively argue that you can do more by working less. For many people in the construction industry, this is a hard concept to embrace. But according to one study, working past the point of fatigue increases problem-solving time by as much as

500%. How many times have you pushed yourself to complete a task only to have to do it all over again the next day? When you are tired, it is much better to take short, focused breaks in order to restore yourself and be more productive. I worked with one company who had a policy that their employees must keep their phones on twenty-four hours a day, seven days a week. I sat in a meeting with one of these employees who answered his phone five times during a one-hour meeting. This may seem like a good thing for customer service, but what is the cost to the employees? What kind of image does this project to other stakeholders? Ask yourself what percentage of phone calls are directly related to your customers' needs. Then ask yourself what percentage of phone calls are low priority time wasters and stress makers. Do you really need to be on call every waking moment?

Many companies are starting to pay attention to this lack of down time and stress related issues and are offering a variety of solutions. Morning exercises stimulate the body and mind. Building in scheduled break times helps employees to be more alert and focused when they return to work. Employees are encouraged to turn off their phones, personal digital assistants, and jobsite radios at these times so they are not constantly bombarded with work. Instead of working through lunches and scheduled breaks, employees are encouraged to have true downtime in order to recover and be more productive.

These group breaks also help with relationships and team-building, creating high performing teams that naturally have higher productivity. By working well together they manage these relationship issues and minimize conflicts that interfere with productivity. They spend less time on non–productive activities and more time on activities that create meaningful results. In other words, they spend much of their time on Quadrant II activities, which are important, but not urgent. Quality and productivity improve when we focus on people, and if productivity rises even by a few percentage points, margins increase dramatically. Take a look at the following example: You have a $25,000,000 project with $10,000,000 in labor costs and $1,000,000 profit. If you improve your productivity by 10%, your labor costs drop to $9,000,000. This would give you a profit of $2,000,000. In other words, with a 10% increase in productivity, you could double your profit!

COMMUNICATION AND KNOWLEDGE SHARING: Knowledge is a firm's most valuable resource. More than 75% of the capitalization of the top companies in the United States is through knowledge and other intangible assets.[16] This is especially true in the construction industry where employee knowledge has great economic value. In fact, in most cases, it is our only competitive edge.

Lack of communication and knowledge management are closely related to poor productivity partly because they stifle innovation and problem solving. Until we tap into the emotional side of these issues, we will be unable to increase knowledge sharing and create true learning organizations. In our courses, we do a warm-up exercise called the Big Egg Drop. We divide into groups and see who can build the least expensive contraption that will catch a raw egg. After this exercise, I ask the question: "If we built this egg catcher again right now, could you build it cheaper, faster, better?" Invariably they say "yes". But isn't this also true of our industry? Although each structure is different, the building components are fairly consistent. Does the knowledge and the lessons learned make their way to each new project? The usual answer is "not very often". Companies who have created lessons-learned databases find out shortly that their use is limited. Why is this? It is because people will only share information with someone they know and trust.

British Petroleum learned this difficult lesson. They spent millions of dollars on knowledge sharing technology, but their employees were still not sharing their knowledge. They finally realized that technology was not the answer. Instead, they cultivated great relationships among their employees, which provided a web of knowledge that was available anytime. As British Petroleum's John Cross puts it, "Since sharing knowledge is important only at the point and time when people need to solve a problem, the key to knowledge management is connecting people in a dialogue."

In fact, some technology may actually hinder productivity. I was talking to the president of a very successful project management software company about this issue. Although they have a great web based software product that provides links for sharing information, some contractors still blame them for the lack of communication on a project. This software company is starting to realize that sharing information is not about the technology. It's about the relationships among the project stakeholders. Some companies have even created the position of knowledge broker to connect people within the company in order to share knowledge more effectively.

If we create these personal connections, if we establish true emotional threads, the employees will be more likely to seek advice and counsel from each other and create true learning organizations. This will ultimately contribute to increased innovation and productivity, higher margins, and a more robust bottom line.

MULTI-CULTURAL ISSUES & WORKING IN OTHER COUNTRIES: We have seen great changes in the cultural makeup of our work force in the past few decades. Many companies are expanding their geographic areas not only in the United States, but internationally. In short, we are encountering many different cultures in this melting pot of construction. How does this affect the way we work? Are we prepared for these diverse cultures with their different values? As companies are finding out, it's not just about learning another language. There are many different aspects of diversity that affect the way we interact and do business.

The United States is made up of many cultures, and they all have different values and unique ways of working. Their sense of time and punctuality, their work ethic and their own set of priorities concerning family, work, and personal time can vary a great deal. They will likely respond differently to situations in the workplace. If companies want to be more effective, they must recognize these cultural differences and try to make adjustments to accommodate them. It may be impossible to accommodate all situations in any given group, but we must make the effort to be aware of these differences and do the best we can.

There are also regional cultures in the United States. Doing business in the north is very different than doing business in the south. In the north, people tend to be more direct and assertive. In the south, this is seen as negative behavior. Southerners refer to these northerners as "Yankees". It is not an affectionate term. Companies in Florida and the west coast tend to have a much more casual workplace than companies in the northeast. These cultural differences must be taken into account when doing business.

These regional differences can be disastrous. One of my old bosses was a "Yankee" from the north and tended to be aggressive and blunt. We were presenting to a school board to build a school in South Georgia. We all drove down from Atlanta with our suits and ties and our well rehearsed, slick, Power Point presentation. When we arrived, the school board greeted us. Their dress was extremely casual. In fact, one of the board members, a farmer in the area, was dressed in overalls. Our "Yankee" lead presenter was blunt and abrasive and talked much too quickly. We came across like a bunch of "city -slickers" with our fancy computer presentation, trying to take advantage of these poor country folk. We would have been better off leaving the "Yankee" at home, dressing casually, establishing rapport with the board, and doing our presentation with posters.

For those companies working internationally, this cultural awareness is even more vital. Working in Europe, Russia, Latin America, and Southeast Asia involves a different set of rules. There are issues with bribery and corruption and other values. In China, "yes" doesn't necessarily mean "yes". It may only mean "I understand what you are saying". In addition, "saving face" is of prime importance. In Russia, you must be prepared to pay a "consultant" who will guide you through the intricacies of working there. In the United States, we tend to be obsessed with time and punctuality. In Latin America, there is a more relaxed view of time. They also value intimate business relationships, which are crucial for successful projects and penetrating new markets.

I facilitated a program with a group of thirty construction managers from Argentina. We had a tight schedule, and I insisted that everyone come back from breaks "on time". The problem was that fifteen minutes past the time to resume, not one person had returned. I was trying to impose my US notion of "on time" on them. I finally got the message and adjusted the schedule based on their culture, because no matter what the consequence, they never came into the room at the scheduled time. I found out that in their culture, "on time" means up to thirty minutes past the agreed upon time. We also created a different daily schedule. In their culture, they tend to start later and finish later. The 6:00 am yoga simply did not work for this group. We started around 9:00 am and did not eat dinner until around 9:00 pm. Making these adjustments when possible allows you to obtain the highest productivity from these different cultures. We must learn to ask ourselves, "Is it wrong or just different?"

Some say business is business the world over, but smart companies are paying attention to the cultural dimensions of the places where they are working by making the necessary adjustments. Lack of understanding of other cultures can turn business triumphs into disasters.

Consider the story of the American entrepreneur who was getting ready to close the deal and sign the contract for a manufacturing facility in Russia. This American was a Mormon and didn't drink alcohol. In Russia, deals are customarily sealed with a vodka toast. The American served soft drinks. Because he did not embrace this honored custom of their culture, the Russians cancelled the deal.

Another cultural disaster took place when a Swedish construction company acquired a company in Poland. Poland, being a former Soviet country, had a very different culture. The bosses were stern and dictatorial. The boss told the workers what to do, and the workers did so without question. The Swedes, on the other hand, were very consensus-driven. They relied on the group to come up with the correct answers. This company sent some Swedish managers to Poland. Not knowing the culture, the Swedish managers had meetings with the Polish workers and asked for their input and ideas. The Polish workers assumed that the Swedes were inept. From their point of view, these foreign managers were so stupid, they were asking the workers to provide the answers! The Swedish managers lost the respect of the workers, and this initial setback took quite some time to overcome.

Where does this lack of understanding originate? Is it a matter of studying cultures, reading history and learning the language?

Those efforts will certainly help, but these misunderstandings go beyond that. With the typical contractor's EQ profile, employees may have an even more difficult time because of their low empathy, low social responsibility, and low interpersonal relationships skills. To be able to navigate these differences, employees must develop these areas. Jonas, a project manager from Sweden, put it this way, "When moving to a new job in a new country I needed to make people feel comfortable to tell me the truth. There were a lot of problems, which needed to be identified and solved. By using emotional intelligence, I think I got a good response, and I could, therefore, take quick action in creating a new structure." Once these emotional skills are improved, it is much easier for employees to see other points of view and establish and maintain good relationships. This is vital for doing business in these culturally diverse workplaces so that we can create more of a team atmosphere and make our workforces more productive. This higher productivity will lead to a less stressful working environment and a better bottom line.

ENVIRONMENTAL ISSUES: According to the United States Green Building Council, the demand for "green" buildings is rising dramatically in the United States and around the world. This increase is fueled by the advantages that green buildings have over conventional construction. The buildings are more energy efficient, conserve water and resources, have lower long-term maintenance costs, and generally last longer than conventional buildings. There is also less exposure to an increasing number of lawsuits related to toxic mold and Sick Building Syndrome.

There are advantages to the occupants as well. Studies show that they are more productive and have less sick days. They experience better indoor air quality, more natural lighting, and more comfortable work environments. In a California study, a school was converted to a day-lit school with the addition of skylights.

After the conversion, the students performed 5 to 14% better on reading, language, and math skills as measured by the California Achievement Test. [17] In a hospital study, surgery patients in rooms with natural lighting needed less pain medication. [18]

This green building trend also has advantages to contractors. By reducing, re-using, and recycling materials, contractors can save a bundle of money on their waste removal costs. As anyone in the construction industry can tell you, these costs are increasing due to limited landfill space and higher tipping fees. I was the Environmental Manager for Skanska USA's Atlanta office when we implemented an environmental management system in order to be certified in ISO 14001, an international environmental standard. During the first year, Skanska's Atlanta office saved over $270,000 in waste removal costs and diverted thousands of cubic yards of waste from landfills.

During the implementation of this system, we encountered some resistance, especially from the guys in the field. They complained that they didn't have time, couldn't train everyone, and didn't have room for recycling dumpsters – the list was endless. What was the source of this resistance? I was at a loss until I began learning about the power of emotional intelligence. Take a look again at the typical construction EQ profile (Chapter 1) and the relatively low scores in social responsibility and empathy. Low scores in these areas indicate that these workers may have difficulty seeing the global picture, the effect of their actions on others, and the interconnectedness of everyone on the planet, which is essential for embracing these environmental concepts.

This green building trend also relates to teamwork. The United States Green Building Council's LEED® (Leadership in Energy & Environmental Design) program is a certification process for green buildings. It takes a high performing team involving all project stakeholders to deliver such a project and receive the certification. Without this sense of team, these green projects are quite difficult to complete.

I worked on a LEED project where the relationships were difficult. The owner hired a construction manager who pitted the architect and designers against the contractor. If the project did not achieve LEED certification, both the architect and the contractor would have to pay liquidated damages. The owner thought that this was the best way to limit his liability, but in fact, it made the LEED process quite difficult. The process became more about blaming each other and shedding risk instead of working together as a team.

Environmental issues can impact a company's image as well. Skanska, a multi-national Swedish contractor, learned this hard lesson at the Halland Ridge Tunnel project in Hallandsås, Sweden. A subcontractor was using a grout containing acrylamide, which contaminated the local groundwater. In the United States, this may have resulted in a small article in the newspaper, but in Sweden, there was a media frenzy surrounding this story. As a result, Skanska's reputation was badly tarnished. They have since overcome this environmental debacle with a stronger focus on environmental issues. The entire company now has an environmental management system, and each business unit is certified in ISO 14001. This focus on environmental issues has improved their image and led to more business opportunities worldwide.

The green building trend is here to stay, and the demand for green buildings will only increase. If you are entering into this market, you will do well to address these emotional intelligence competencies prior to any technical training. This will give your people the tools they need to be able to understand and implement these green building strategies, improve your company's image, and capture more of this emerging market. This will, in turn, create opportunities for business and eventually increase the bottom line.

HUMAN RESOURCE PROCESSES such as hiring, review processes, turnover, training, retention, and succession planning:

Hiring and Recruiting: New research has determined that a bad hire can cost as much as twice their annual salary. Yet most companies continue to make the same hiring mistakes. For someone who makes an annual salary of $80,000, the costs for making a poor hire can run upward to $160,000!

Most companies to whom we have talked have insufficient processes in place for recruiting and hiring. These processes consist mainly of impromptu interviews. Few, if any of the managers have been trained in interviewing techniques. The lack of effective hiring processes can be costly.

A leader at a top 50 contractor here in the United States confided to me that they end up hiring "the best of the worst". Companies can make better decisions by determining what skills are required for each position and whether or not the candidate possesses those skills. A great way to match these skills is by using the EQ-i® evaluation. Before, it was difficult to measure soft skills such as empathy and interpersonal relationship skills during the interview process. Now we can measure these traits and make better hiring decisions.

Recently, we received a call from an extended stay hotel company who was interviewing for a mid level management position. After an initial interview, they had some concern about the candidate's interpersonal skills, and there were indications that this person may be a micromanager. So they decided to invest in an EQ-i® evaluation. The evaluation showed that the candidate had good interpersonal skills, but showed relatively low flexibility and low self-regard along with high problem solving skills, which could manifest itself in the form of micromanaging.

We recommended some behavioral type interview questions to make sure that these areas would not be a problem. To address the flexibility and potential control issues, the company asked, "We value letting our employees stretch themselves in their positions. Can you tell us about a time in your work history where you had to be very flexible and let subordinates do things their own way?" According to the company's managers, using the EQ profile was a great way to avoid hiring the wrong person. And companies who avoid making bad hires will save money.

Review Processes & Retention: Can you remember when people worked for the same company for their entire careers? This is no longer true. According to the United States Department of Labor, voluntary turnover rates are on the rise. A recent article in Engineering News Record discussed the high cost of turnover. Catherine Santee, Senior Vice President of Finance for CH2M Hill stated, "All of us are fighting for talent." Michael Creed, CEO of McKim and Creed added, "We've finally realized we're in the people business."[19]

According to a 2003 Mercer Survey, half of the companies surveyed reported that their employees receive little or no ongoing performance management training and very little ongoing feedback and communication. Most contractors do not have meaningful review processes that discuss career goals and developmental needs, while some companies have no review process in place at all. Without these reviews, employees tend to feel unappreciated and disengaged. According to the Gallup Organization, most people leave companies because of poor treatment from their immediate supervisor. Many times, this poor treatment manifests itself in a lack of appreciation. If companies improve the EQ of their supervisors and teach them to create a meaningful dialogue with their employees, the employees will feel valued and appreciated, and their level of engagement will increase. According the ISR, a research and consulting firm, high engagement companies improved their operating incomes by 19.2 percent while low engagement companies declined 32.7 percent during the study period. Managers can engage employees by discussing their developmental needs and helping them to improve. Managers can also use the information for succession planning by determining what competencies are required for future positions, then helping the employee to measure and improve them. If employees know there is a plan for their future, they will naturally be more engaged. Some employers use training programs to honor and reward their star employees.

If we ignore our employees, if we let them stagnate, if we don't offer them a plan for their careers, we will be faced with ever-rising turnover rates and unproductive, unmotivated, disengaged employees. But if we use emotional intelligence to develop managers and employees, to make them more valuable, and to address personal development issues, they will feel appreciated. They will value the company who provides this type of personal development and will be much less likely to look elsewhere for employment.

Succession Planning: One of our clients, an engineering firm, has a succession plan that ensures continuity. The two people directly under the CEO are in line for the CEO's position. These positions are thoughtfully filled with the next leaders of the company. When these two heirs apparent took the EQi, we identified some areas that they could work on in order to be able to eventually step into the CEO role some day. This organization realized that the skills these individuals utilize now are not the same skills that they will need to run the company. This kind of evaluation and purposeful development for key positions is essential for good succession planning and successful leadership.

Another big issue in the construction industry is stalled

career paths. It happens time and time again. When a technically trained or educated person is adept at managing processes, they are promoted. They keep getting promoted until they are no longer managing processes, but managing people. And that is when things tend to go awry. They believe themselves to be intelligent and may have highly developed technical knowledge and expertise. Some even have post graduate degrees in their fields. So why can't they manage people?

This frustration often leads to burnout or even worse, demotion or termination. I've seen it enough times to say that it is a trend, indicating a definite need to teach these potential leaders the "soft skills" needed to break through these career barriers.

Another issue associated with succession planning is filling those middle management positions. Most companies have talented young people and seasoned veterans, but there is a dearth of good, qualified, middle managers. The thing that is usually missing from these young managers is the maturity and the people skills needed to step into leadership positions. By focusing on their emotional intelligence, we can teach them people skills and transition them into leadership positions in a shorter period of time.

Recently, the CEO for a top 50 contractor asked, "What if these guys don't improve their interpersonal skills? Do we fire them?" The short answer is that we must try to match the skills to the position. If an employee continues to have low scores in interpersonal skills, despite continued efforts in training and development, you may be able to find a position where these skills are less important, where they don't have as much interaction with key stakeholders. Putting people in the right place to make them more comfortable and productive is essential for increasing overall productivity and the bottom line.

Training and Development: Is your company wasting money

on training and development? Training, for most companies, is about as effective as rearranging the deck chairs on the Titanic. Daniel Goleman refers to corporate training programs as the "Billion Dollar Mistake". 20 Actually, in the United States, the cost could be much higher than that. According to the American Society for Training and Development, corporations in the United States spend $109 billion annually on training. You would think that spending money on training would be a good thing. But is it?

Most training is event based and informational. Participants come to a training event and are given loads of information, usually in the form of a lecture or Power Point presentation. Normally, there is very little follow-up or coaching. I call these training events "three-ring binder" programs. I'm sure you've attended programs where you listen to an eight-hour lecture and take your three-ring binder home, only to forget what you learned and go back to your normal routine in a few days. You put your three-ring binder on a shelf, and a year later, when you need the binder, you take out the contents and throw them away. This approach to training is ineffective to say the least.

The Vice President of a Federal bank recently told me of an internal group that had horrible communication, personality conflicts, and rampant gossip. They lacked the ability to function well as a team. When I asked about her assessment of the situation, she told me that they were sending them to a ropes course. Now I have nothing against ropes courses. They can be quite entertaining and may ease the superficial issues of such a group for a short period of time. But the underlying issues are never addressed, much less resolved. The group members tend to revert back to their old ways within a few days.

If you take a group of construction folks with the typical construction manager's emotional intelligence profile, and try to teach them some type of interpersonal skill, they may not have the emotional makeup or the right tools to be able to implement what you are trying to teach them. The wiser strategy is to start with an evaluation of their emotional intelligence. This will not only provide a foundation from which to work, but it will allow you to target specific areas for development. You will have laid the proper foundation to ensure that all future training will be applied in a meaningful way. In addition, it is vital to include coaching and follow-up. Without accountability, it is human nature to set these development strategies aside.

Companies can now stop throwing money away on training that is soon forgotten. By using this EQ methodology to evaluate, measure, and improve these emotional competencies, and by utilizing ongoing coaching and follow-up, companies can create fundamental change from within instead of imparting information that will never be applied. See the appendix for case studies and documentation that supports this training methodology to create behavioral change.

4 : Frequently Asked Questions

I sn't this just another one of those personality profiles?
Invariably, several program participants tell us they've already
taken all of these kinds of tests and that this is nothing new.
Many of them have taken the Myers-Briggs or the DISC test.
There are literally thousands of these tests on the market today.
Most are based on preferences – you know the types of questions
– would you rather read a book or sail a boat? For people with low
self-awareness, this can be very informative and fun, but most of
these tests are rather limited for detailed, personal development.
For those who are somewhat self-aware, these tests are merely
confirmations of what they already know. In fact, the common
response is, "Yep, that's me. So what?" A construction company I
worked for used the DISC profile for all of its employees. DISC
is a test that indicates the following personality archetypes:

Dominant	Tends to be direct and guarded
Interactive	Tends to be direct and open
Steady	Tends to be indirect and open
Compliance	Tends to be indirect and guarded

As it turned out, 80% of the people in our construction company were "Dominants". What does that tell you? Most people
in the construction business have a dominant style. They tend
to be direct and guarded. Didn't we know that already?

Myers-Briggs, another personality test, indicates the following traits:

Extraversion	versus	*Introversion*	E or I
Sensing	versus	*iNtuition*	S or N
Thinking	versus	*Feeling*	T or F
Judging	versus	*Perceiving*	J or P

When you take the test, you are given a Myers-Briggs Personality Type. But what are you supposed to do with that information? There are some Myers-Briggs modules on teambuilding

and how to deal with other Myers-Briggs types, but how do you know the personality type of everyone you encounter? One company made everyone put their Myers-Briggs profile on their coffee cups, but this concept was a miserable failure.

Let's a look at Case Study 5, the thirty-year-old financial consultant who could not keep a job (see appendix).

CASE STUDY 5

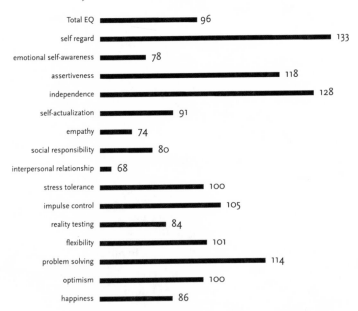

Total EQ	96
self regard	133
emotional self-awareness	78
assertiveness	118
independence	128
self-actualization	91
empathy	74
social responsibility	80
interpersonal relationship	68
stress tolerance	100
impulse control	105
reality testing	84
flexibility	101
problem solving	114
optimism	100
happiness	86

We can see from this case study that "a very high independence score and a very low interpersonal relationship score suggests that she is a loner, perhaps due to a serious inability to relate to others. Moreover, her difficulty in empathizing with others contributes to this inability to relate to people and to feel part of the larger social context."

When this woman took the Myers-Briggs, she was an ESFJ (Extraverted Feeling with Introverted Sensing). But the results of the Myers-Briggs gave her little information about why she could not hold a job. After taking the EQ-i®, she could target specific areas for development that helped in her pursuit of a career.

With personality tests, your results rarely change throughout your life. In the DISC profile, if you are a Dominant, you will probably be a Dominant until you die. In the Myers-Briggs, if you are an ESFJ, you will probably be an ESFJ until you die. The EQ-i® is a very different tool. It measures specific competencies such as empathy, assertiveness, and problem solving skills. Once you choose areas to develop, a detailed development plan is created utilizing specific development strategies. There is practical application, measurement and improvement. This creates fundamental behavioral shifts. Personality tests simply do not do that.

Is there a correlation between emotional intelligence & performance?
I facilitated a program for a top 100 contractor based in the southern United States using emotional intelligence as a foundation for leadership development. After the managers were evaluated, I ranked their interpersonal scores (empathy, social responsibility, and interpersonal relationship skills) from the highest to the lowest. This company had their own ranking system in order to identify their star performers, the ones who contributed most to the success of the company. The astonishing fact was that the company's overall ranking and the ranking of interpersonal skills correlated almost one to one. This told us that the managers who had the best interpersonal skills were also the company's stars. They were the managers involved in the most profitable projects who contributed the most to the company's bottom line. Multi-Health Systems has a program called Star Performer where companies look at the EQ-i® profiles of their star performers for particular departments or positions and determine which emotional competencies are essential for high performance. Then it is just a matter of recruiting, hiring, and training for those competencies.

Can emotional intelligence be learned?

Seabiscuit was just a broken down horse incapable of winning until someone saw his potential and developed it through training. It was only then that he became one of the greatest racehorses in the history of racing. The trick is to be able to identify individual potential and develop it with effective techniques. But how do you teach something like empathy? We have developed a methodology targeted for the construction industry called "Emotional Intelligence – Foundation for Your Future". It was co-developed with Kate Cannon, a pioneer in the field of emotional intelligence.

After the initial EQ evaluation and feedback, we begin with a half-day program where each participant creates a detailed, individual development plan. The participant targets specific competencies based on their future needs and then chooses development strategies from different categories depending on their learning style. We utilize many different types of exercises and development ideas and use various media such as books, fables, movies, operas, plays, and websites. We also emphasize the day-to-day application of this learning and provide inspirational quotes for each competency. But the key to this learning is in the follow-up and coaching. We contact individuals every three or four weeks to check on their progress, offer encouragement, and provide coaching. Without this individual coaching and follow-up, the participants tend to set aside their development plans. But if they know they will be re-evaluated and that someone will be checking in with them every few weeks, they are much more likely to work on their development plans and create fundamental behavioral change from within. One participant said this about the process, "I thought that people are who they are by their mid-twenties. I definitely feel that people are capable of significant change."

We have an empathy exercise that is extremely effective. Keep in mind that most of our participants are men. We instruct each participant to go home from work, dismiss the children, turn off the television, sit their wife down and ask her to tell him about her day. He cannot solve any of her problems, offer any suggestions, or make any comments during her monologue. The only thing he is supposed to do is try to understand the feelings she experienced throughout the day. The only comment he can offer is "that must have made you feel …" After the wives overcome the initial shock of this, they are quite pleased. In fact, several participants reported a spark of romance after this session. Talk about positive reinforcement for developing your empathy skills! Once the participants can tap into the power of empathy, they are motivated to apply it in the workplace. By truly listening and putting themselves in the shoes of subcontractors, owners, architects, and other project stakeholders, they find that they are much more effective in their day-to-day dealings with them.

I love to tell the story of Bryan, a superintendent in his late thirties with an anger problem. He told me that this problem troubled him since he was young, and that if I could help him find a way to control it, he would be most grateful. This issue showed up in his EQ-i®. He had low emotional self-awareness along with high assertiveness and low impulse control. His low emotional self-awareness didn't allow him to feel himself getting angry, and eventually, with his low impulse control, it just boiled over. The first thing we did was work on his emotional self-awareness. I suggested that he try to become aware of where he felt anger in his body and identify it as early as possible. We also worked on basic breathing and meditation techniques along with centering techniques to help with his impulse control. I gave him a book to read and told him that it may be a little "out there" for him, but to try and find something he could relate to.

In the process of reading the book, he found a centering technique that worked for him. He created a focal point by putting a photograph of his two small girls on his mobile phone. When he felt himself getting frustrated, (with greater emotional self awareness, he felt it in his body), he excused himself from the situation, took ten deep breaths, flipped open his phone, and looked at his little girls. This allowed him to decompress and control his anger. In his words, "Leaving a bad situation, even briefly, has allowed me to not act in anger or impulsively." He improved his emotional management and changed his behavior, making him a more effective leader. With this shift, he has learned to listen more without being so reactive. He told me that the people who work with him have noticed these changes. As he puts it, "Listening, not reacting to people I encounter has led to a more positive approach to my professional life." In addition to improved leadership skills, there has also been an improvement in his health and well-being. He is less stressed and better able to handle difficult situations without compromising his health.

Even if the scores from the EQ-i® do not increase; there still can be some very useful information for the participant. Annelise, a purchasing manager from Denmark, decided to work on her social responsibility, which was relatively low. Eleven months later, at the end of the program, when she took the EQ-i® again, she found that her social responsibility score was even lower. Interestingly enough, her self-actualization, happiness, and optimism had increased dramatically. When we discussed these numbers, I asked her why she chose to work on social responsibility. She told me that she believed that it was the right thing to do, that she thought her family and friends wanted her to spend more time with them. I asked her if she had spent more time with family and friends in an effort to increase her social responsibility. She replied that she had not. She told me that work had been particularly hectic, and she had been working non-stop since the beginning of the program. She usually worked alone rather than in groups or teams. She also indicated that she felt a little guilty for working so much.

I asked her if she enjoyed working and she responded by saying that it was the most important thing in her life. She loved the challenge and felt that the company needed her during this particularly difficult period, which made her feel valued and important. That was the reason for her significant increases in self-actualization, happiness, and optimism. I suggested that perhaps this second evaluation revealed that during this period in her life, her work, which gives her great joy, is something that she would do well to focus on. In addition, since she worked alone, this way of working did not contribute to increasing her social responsibility. This conversation was a great relief to her. Perhaps all she needed was permission to enjoy her work life without guilt. So, in this case, although the competency she had originally chosen decreased, the results of the second EQ-i® gave us some real insights into the direction she wanted for her personal and professional life.

Isn't this just another management fad?
I have given much thought and introspection to this question. As a matter of fact, I considered this possibility when I first started this work. But after seeing the results and seeing the supporting data, the answer to this question is a resounding NO! The shelves are filled with thousands of self-help books for managers. And many of these books contain good information. So, why do management fads come and go like the tides? Because there is a fundamental flaw in their application. They pile generic information on top of generic problems without regard to the individual. No matter how good the information is or how valid the approach, without addressing the fundamental emotional makeup of the individual, the application of this information may never take place.

Every company we have worked with agrees that communication is essential in the construction industry. Companies spend millions of dollars on training to give their people better communication skills. But because of the typical EQ profiles of most people in the construction industry, they are often incapable of applying this training. If they have high assertiveness, independence, and self-regard, and low empathy and interpersonal relationship skills, they will likely come across as someone who doesn't listen, won't ask for other's opinions, and does whatever they think is best regardless of any group input. You can put that person in a communication seminar or buy them books to teach them how to communicate, but it is very probable that they will still be unable to communicate effectively when the seminar is over.

If someone has low flexibility and optimism, they may have issues concerning change. This person can go to a seminar on change management or read a book like "Who Moved My Cheese?", but his lack of flexibility usually prevents him from truly embracing change. He will have difficulty in the construction industry because of the constant change, but if his flexibility and optimism are increased, he will be much better able to deal with this issue.

Using emotional intelligence as the foundation for development programs is a different approach. Instead of starting with a particular area of training such as communication or teambuilding, we address the fundamental emotional developmental needs of every individual. Then we address these needs with specific, targeted learning modules. By addressing the emotional competencies first, the participants can develop the emotional makeup to be able to apply the concepts of the learning modules. All future training can be related back to the employees' emotional intelligence development plans, which also make any subsequent company training more effective.

5 : *How Do We Get There From Here?*
A step-by-step methodology for improving emotional intelligence

Things do not change; we change.
—Henry David Thoreau

We have learned many lessons from these programs over the years. We have learned what works and what does not work. We have developed a very good methodology that is highly successful. Here is the step-by-step process.

1   Learn more about emotional intelligence. There are many books on the subject. Discuss the basics & the options.

2   Choose a consultant. Be sure that you choose someone who is certified to administer evaluations and give feedback. It is also important that the consultant understand your business and the way emotional intelligence relates to improving it.

3   Choose an evaluation tool. The Bar-On EQ-i® is an excellent self-assessment tool, but there are several very good tools on the market. MSCEIT® is another instrument that measures EQ. The difference is that MSCEIT® is an ability based EQ evaluation instead of a self-assessment. You may choose to do a 360 evaluation where the employee measures his own EQ, and subordinates, peers, bosses, clients, family, and friends evaluate him as well.

4   Start with the top management. Then move on to a group of managers in your company whom you believe will benefit from this type of work. The selection process should be well thought out, and the participants should be given a quick overview of emotional intelligence prior to taking the EQi®.

5   Have participants take the evaluation and receive individual feedback. Make it clear that these evaluations are confiden-

tial and will not be shared with anyone in the company. We emphasize that the EQi® is a snapshot in time, and ask each participant to think about what they need going forward personally and professionally.

6 Have each participant create a detailed development plan. This preliminary work will give participants a better understanding of themselves, their limitations, and what to work on. We have developed a module called Emotional Intelligence – Foundation for Your Future, which discusses what emotional intelligence is, why it is important, and how to develop it.

7 Determine the group scores and address any group developmental needs. For the construction industry, these needs usually lie in the area of interpersonal skills. Reinforce this emotional intelligence learning process with learning modules such as communication skills, relationships skills, teambuilding, negotiation skills, coaching, and motivation. Teach the group about stress management and time management. These learning modules may also include areas specific to the company or group such as business strategies and vision.

The programs we provide are truly customized to each individual, to each group, and to each company. And with minimal lecture and self-directed, experiential learning, each program is truly unique.

8 Spread out the learning process. This type of emotional learning takes place in a different part of the brain than cognitive learning. It's not like solving a problem. It is more like learning a language or learning to play a musical instrument. It takes repetition and internalization over a longer period of time. We recommend a minimum of nine months to one year.

9 Coach the participants during the learning process. This

ongoing coaching will reinforce the learning and hold the participants accountable for implementing their development plans.

10 Have the participants retake the EQ-i® evaluation and receive individual feedback. Discuss the changes in the scores and what they mean as well as the individual's EQ development plan and behavioral changes.

11 Provide a wrap-up session where participants discuss their before and after scores and what they mean in terms of their development. Celebrate the accomplishments and analyze the shortfalls, then end with a discussion of how to create lifelong learning. Re-evaluate the development plans and modify accordingly.

12 Have the participants check in annually to see where they are in their development. Their professional and personal situations may have changed, and they may need to focus on different areas. They should be re-evaluated and receive individual feedback as a part of the follow-up procedure.

13 At this point, the participants may need more coaching & reinforced learning modules to address new areas of learning.

LESSONS LEARNED: There are several errors that companies have made with regard to this emotional intelligence work. In order to avoid these mistakes, be aware of the following:

1. It is a good idea to take top managers through this type of evaluation and training first. Make sure this work is aligned with the company vision and values. We had one participant who told his boss he was working on empathy. His boss replied, "No you're not." His boss thought that empathy equated to weakness and this company was not going to show weakness. You don't want participants to return to their jobs to find resistance to these emotional intelligence concepts. If they are working to improve

their interpersonal skills while senior managers are neglecting theirs, they will be frustrated. Senior management must know what this work is and support it fully.

I talked to one company that I thought would be a good fit for this type of work. They had a daycare center in their offices. When I gave my pitch to the HR manager, he told me that he didn't think the company would embrace this emotional intelligence work. I asked him about the daycare center, and he told me that the only reason they had a daycare center was because it encouraged the employees to work longer hours. With this type of company value-work extremely hard until you have a heart attack and die-emotional intelligence simply won't work.

2. Be sure to include follow-up and coaching in the program. When there is no follow-up, participants treat the program as another one of those training programs that wastes their time and yields little practical results. When you work with each individual to create a development plan, coach them through it, and follow up with a second evaluation and interview, it encourages accountability and gives the program credibility. And when the participants know there will be follow-up, they are much more likely to work on their plans and create fundamental behavioral change from within.

3. Don't be discouraged if all of the participants don't embrace this work. It takes some time to win the skeptical construction folks over, but in the end, nearly all embrace this work and create that fundamental change. There will be some who will never value emotional intelligence work. In our experience, this is less than 5% of the participants. But even these who don't participate fully seem to get something out of the program and find at least one thing that helps them in their life and career.

4. Make sure that the style of teaching is effective for the group. We use a maximum of 20% lecture and Power Point.

The other 80% is experiential learning, self-directed learning, group discussions, role-plays, and hands-on exercises. We take great pains to understand the company's business objectives and make sure the learning is practical and applicable.

5. Many training companies are repackaging their canned training programs and referring to them as programs on "emotional intelligence." Let the buyer beware. Make sure your consultants are qualified. Check their credentials and their certifications. Ask for references and focus on past results. Make sure that their evaluation instruments are validated. One of my colleagues refers to these un-validated tests as "Ladies Home Journal" tests. Although they can be entertaining, they should not be used for personal development.

6 : Final Thoughts

My wife and I were in Amsterdam and took in a concert at a very famous concert hall called the Consertgebouw. We heard Nigel Kennedy, a brilliant violinist, but quite different from any violinist we had seen before. He wore his hair in a spiky Mohawk. He wore boots and a silk coat unlike the members in the orchestra, who all had white ties and tails. The first thing he did was take down the velvet ropes that separated the audience from the orchestra. With a great flourish, he said, "Now we are united!"

During the concert, he acted more like a rock and roll star than a classical violinist. He rocked back and forth with orchestra members and danced around the stage. At one point, he walked off stage while playing and came back on kicking a soccer ball. Continuing to play, he kicked the ball out into the audience. It was a delight watching his passion and his great musical ability.

At the end of the concert, I leaned over to my wife and said, "I want to be that guy. I want to be that weird guy who is passionate about what he does and gets great results even though people look at him as someone who is a little bit out there." She thought a minute and said, "You teach emotional intelligence, yoga, and meditation to contractors. I think you are that guy."

I understand the reluctance of the people in the construction industry to embrace this work because it is so far outside their comfort zones. I probably won't grow a Mohawk, but I will continue this work with passion and enthusiasm because I truly believe that emotional intelligence can transform companies and change people's lives.

We have been grappling with these construction industry problems for decades, perhaps centuries. Isn't it time we focused on the root causes of these problems and addressed them head on? When I saw the connection between the typical emotional intelligence profiles and the major industry problems, I felt like Marlon Brando's character, Walter Kurtz, in the movie Apocalypse Now. I had this sudden insight "like a diamond in the middle of my forehead."

If companies begin to realize that people are their most precious resource, if they are willing to take a chance and use this incredible tool called emotional intelligence, they will begin to hire the right people, nurture them, promote their personal development, give them direction for their careers, plan for succession, decrease turnover rates, and increase retention. In addition, this will facilitate increased customer service, teamwork, and productivity. In turn, accidents, stress, and burnout will decrease. Companies that embrace this work will improve the industry image so that young people will flock to our ranks, and our sons and daughters will carry on this proud tradition of contracting. What's the alternative? If we let things continue as they are, the industry may be in trouble. Our inaction could cripple construction, but our focus on people will lead us to lasting solutions.

These types of problems are not limited to the construction industry. In fact, most industries are encountering these issues. All industries can benefit from this EQ methodology by focusing more on the human factor. When you get right down to it, business is all about people. And people are all about emotional intelligence. Let's put the people dimension back into our business. Let's make the phrase "people are our most important asset" more than just a slogan. Your employees are your only long-term, competitive advantage. Companies must pay attention to the people-profit connection. Because if companies take care of their people, people will take care of their companies, and profits will soar.

Appendix: Case Studies

Case Study 1
Summary Report for
Leadership Development Program 2006

Prepared by
G. Brent Darnell
Brent Darnell & Associates, Inc.

This is a report with results from a Leadership Development Program for the year 2006. The Company elected to maintain anonymity because they believed that this work with emotional intelligence was a competitive advantage. The Company is a top 100 general contractor. There were twenty-two program participants consisting of nine superintendents, two senior project managers, five project managers, two assistant project managers, two pre-construction managers, and two construction managers. The program ran from February to November 2006. The participants took the initial EQ-i® in February 2006. There were six learning modules spread throughout the year consisting of the following:
1. EQ-Foundation for your Future
2. Management/Time Management
3. Teambuilding
4. Coaching and Mentoring
5. Communication and Presentation
6. Relationships and Creating Lifelong Learning

Prior to the last learning module, the participants retook the EQ-i® and received individual feedback. Throughout the program, the participants received ongoing coaching and feedback a minimum of every three or four weeks via email and phone.

This continuing dialogue between the participants and the coach allowed the group to stay focused on their goals and be accountable for their personal development plans.

EXECUTIVE SUMMARY:

Out of the 22 employees originally enrolled in the course, one participant left the Company and one participant did not graduate because he missed a number of key classes. The following data and quotes are from the remaining 20 participants. All participants filled out the final questionnaire, some divulged their names and some filled it out anonymously.

Overall, according to the program participants, the program was beneficial. To the question, "Would you recommend this program to others?" everyone answered "Yes".

The results from the before and after EQi group scores (see next page) can be affected by many things-life changes, present job situations, career changes, and even the state of mind of the participant while they took the evaluation. Although several of the participants decreased certain areas of their EQi scores, most increased in the areas on which they were working, and some increased dramatically. According to the statistician at MHS, the publisher of the EQi evaluation, increases of five points or more can indicate fairly significant behavioral shifts.

The first thing we notice is that the group's total EQ increased by 12, which approaching a standard deviation, which is statistically very significant. The first total EQ number was 101, which is only one point above the mean, but now, as a group, they are into the above average range. Please also note that before the course, seven of the seventeen competencies measured were at or below the mean (100). After the course, there were no competencies below the mean (100). Before the course, there were no competencies that were in the above average range (> 110). After the course, there were 7 competencies in the above average range.

GROUP AVERAGES — BEFORE (▪) & AFTER (■)

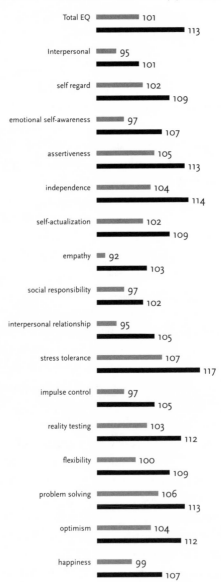

THE PEOPLE-PROFIT CONNECTION

Note that their interpersonal composite scale (empathy, social responsibility and interpersonal relationships) scores increased by 6 points, which indicates behavioral change.

Note the dramatic increases in several key areas: emotional self awareness (better understanding of self, +10), independence (+10), empathy (better understanding of others, +11), interpersonal relationships (the ability to establish and maintain relationships, +10), stress tolerance (the ability to handle stresses, +10), reality testing (+9), and flexibility (+9). Also, note that all other competencies increased by varying amounts, the smallest of which was social responsibility (+5). The scores indicate that the group is much more aware of their own emotions, which is the first step toward good emotional management. They are also better at relationships and more empathetic toward others. The scores also indicate that they are more flexible (increased flexibility), take a more systematic approach to solving problems (increased reality testing and problem solving), and are somewhat happier and self satisfied than when they first took the EQi in February of 2006 (self actualization, happiness, and optimism increases). In addition, even though they still live in a world of chaos according to their group profile (high stress tolerance and relatively low impulse control) they are better able to handle their stress. The large increase in independence and smaller increase in social responsibility may require monitoring to ensure that the group doesn't become too independent. Also, the Company should keep reinforcing the need for good interpersonal skills to offset the increase in assertiveness.

There were many participants with outstanding results, but there were two that made exceptional progress and changed their behaviors significantly. One vastly improved his stress management and health, quit smoking, lost weight, and really turned things around mentally and physically. He had increases in some areas of three standard deviations, which is quite remarkable.

There was another participant, we'll call him Bill, who showed an initial reluctance to work on his low areas. He insisted that his job performance was excellent. And it was. I explained to him that I wasn't here to fix him because he wasn't broken. My job was to try and find ways to make him more effective. I asked him to share his EQ-i* evaluation with people he trusted, and ask them if they thought he could benefit by embracing this work.

The more he thought about it, the more he was convinced that this would help his life and his career. So he made up his mind to give this emotional intelligence idea a try. Once he understood the concepts, he became highly committed to his personal development. He read dozens of books, applied the learning each day, and brought his entire project team in on the process of helping him to improve. After about six months, during one of our follow-up discussions, I asked him if others had noticed any behavioral shifts in him. He asked his superiors to let me know if they had noticed any changes. His supervisor sent me the following email. "Bill has worked with me since 1998, and the recent changes are nothing less than remarkable. Since starting with our Company, his ability and potential were obvious, but Bill resisted the necessary behavioral changes required to realize his potential. In the past, Bill struggled to maintain working relationships with individuals that did not display his level of commitment and was not understanding of those with lesser abilities. This created a lot of friction over the years as Bill's work ethic, determination, and ability are not easily matched. He is starting a new project as lead superintendent, and I think this will be Bill's opportunity to prove to all that he is truly one of our very best." Another superior added "I completely agree. Bill has really turned it around. I think he is a future star."

FEEDBACK QUESTIONNAIRE SUMMARY: We asked the participants to fill out a detailed questionnaire at the end of the program to gage the overall effectiveness. Here is a summary of their answers:

1. *What have you learned about yourself during this course?*

"That I don't spend much time for myself."

"I am too impulsive and need to work on empathy."

"I have a tendency to be a bit overbearing, but I improve in many areas by sitting back and listening to what other people have to say."

"Becoming aware of your own and other people's emotions makes you a powerful person."

"I can change behaviors and traits that seemed permanent with small, consistent efforts."

"That being assertive is only a small part of what makes me successful at my job."

"I thought that people are who they are by their mid 20s. I definitely feel that people are capable of significant change."

"More patience and self control, which has made me more effective."

"That you can have significant changes in behavior, and practicing various items will affect change in others."

"I've learned that by being cognizant of my emotions I can more effectively communicate with others and am more willing to actually listen and retain what is being communicated to me."

"The value of emotional intelligence, that there is no shame in being aware of your feelings."

"That I *can* change. It's not as difficult to open myself up, look inside, and see myself as others might see me. Then, improve myself."

"I am much more aware of what is going on around me and how it affects others."

2. *What practical things have you learned from this course?*
"Emotional self-awareness is critical."

"To listen more."

"To hold my anger in check and not be so quick to lash out."

"It's all about relationships and how we interact with others. That is what makes us successful or unsuccessful."

"Practical applications have been used in several different situations. I use the lesson of telling something personal to get an architect, engineer, or subcontractor to get them emotionally invested."

"The ability to understand what makes people tick and use that to improve my communication skills."

"Do not always say what is exactly on your mind. Also you need to read people properly to find out how you need to respond to them."

"Patience and listening lead to self control. Self control leads to more understanding, better relationships, and more positive outcomes without wasting time or interjecting useless heartaches."

"To slow down and think about what is going on around me."

"In complex construction projects, you will not be successful if your first tool for conflict resolution is to beat everyone involved."

"How to take reflection time each day, how to improve my presentation skills, and how to make educated group decisions."

"Awareness of the importance of listening, dedicated to feeling others' 'pain' to allow better understanding, and the importance of non-verbal communication.

3. *How have you applied that learning to your day to day professional life?*

"Show genuine concern-how can I help you do your job?"

"I calmly listen to subcontractors, owners, and design team concerns and place myself in their shoes before responding to requests and accusations.

"Owner relationships, subcontractor conflict resolution, team building within the the Company team."

"Better communication with my team and subcontractors without making it personal."

"Calmer, more positive approaches have helped lead to a generally more relaxed demeanor, and this has resulted in much more positive response from others."

"Handle myself better in meetings, better relationships with owners and subcontractors, and improved problem solving skills."

"In order to be more effective you must first listen, then set a plan of action."

"Have lowered the number of outbursts which made me listen to all of the various points of view before making a decision."

"I have learned to keep my anger in check and I am getting more out of my subcontractors on the job."

"The course has helped open my eyes and see things differently."

4. *Can you think of specific instances (personally and/or professionally) where you reacted differently as a result of this course and handled a situation for a better outcome?*

"Not a specific instance, but I'm not sure if I would still be here without this course. The older I've gotten, the less tolerant I have been to stress. But this course has allowed me to re-develop my ability to cope with stress and still maintain happiness and self-regard."

"The course helped my take control of my office when others were being negative and disruptive."

"I was able to see the owner's perspective, which helped me understand that he isn't always out to get the Company."

"More interaction with weakest subcontractors, understanding how they fail can help resolve current and future problems."

"Too many to name."

"Every schedule meeting I've had within the last 6 months."

"By finding something personal to talk about with a hard nosed steel subcontractor (the military), I worked my way out of a change order."

"I use the cross generational training a lot in my day to day dealings. When we first did the class, I thought it was not on target, but the more I looked at how they react to things, I really started to manage them differently."

"Received a letter from a subcontractor about "demands for settlement". I calmly addressed each item and we reached a fair compromise. My usual fear of seeming 'weak' by my staff by not beating the subcontractor into submission did not concern me."

"Dealing with subcontractors as people instead of broken cogs in the construction machine, developing one on one relationships with team members, determining where people are coming from prior to acting on short term goal."

"There was a subcontractor who thought that he was owed something that we didn't give him. I took the time to sit down with a subcontractor and go over everything with him. He came to the same conclusion without me having to tell him that he was wrong."

"During a recent meeting with a subcontractor that got off to a rough start, I used some of the techniques learned in the class, got everyone calmed down, and worked out a manageable solution."

"During weekly subcontractor coordination meetings, monthly OAC (Owner/Architect/Contractor) meetings, and daily design team discussions, I try to incorporate the guiding principles of listening before speaking. It has definitely helped me on both a personal and professional basis."

"Giving the owner the benefit of the doubt, and as far as possible, giving him the outcome he was looking for. He is happy as a result and continues to praise our management and their efforts."

5. *Do you think these types of courses will help the Company's business? If so, how?*

Everyone answered in the affirmative. Some specific comments:

"Improves client relationships."

"By learning how to distinguish what makes you tick and how others react to that, this course will help dozens of the Company's employees establish, cultivate, and maintain relationships and good business practices that can only increase the Company's intrinsic value."

"Everyone builds for essentially the same costs. Those who manage the relationships the best will ultimately win."

"It will help with how to deal with subcontracts to labor, on how we speak and react to all of our personnel and to have a smoother running job."

"Future negotiated work is easier to develop with people who like you."

"These courses will help as respect and rational thought governs work, not yelling and emotion."

"It can help our future leaders be more professional and aware of the thoughts and feelings of our clients."

"I've seen amazing reactions, especially from some of the

younger class members in finding their own weak points, analyzing how to fix them, and moving forward with a definite plan on how to improve. This will make them much more effective managers in the long run."

"I think it improves things internally and externally. It's a benefit to me as a manager and I feel it really helps some of the field guys who may not have had the education background as some others. It also gives them something extra to pull from. Externally it helps with negotiations with subcontractors along with relationship building with owners."

"Communication is the blood of a Company. If you can master it, you're in business."

"It drastically improved communication and negotiating skills and the ability to relate to other people resulting in better relationships with clients, architects, and subcontractors. It also improved planning and organizational skills."

"These courses will help to soften or make our leaders be better listeners and be more empathetic. This is the true tool of the problem solver."

"These courses will give the Company more balanced employees who work smarter."

"This course was very effective in maintaining better relationships in the industry."

"Contractors need to understand that today's economy doesn't support always being hard on subcontractors and consultants. Trying to align your goals will help more in the long run."

"By fostering better relationships with owners, architects, engineers, subcontractors, and suppliers I believe we will receive better prices from subcontractors and suppliers and get more repeat work from owners."

"The course helps us accept, recognize, and then work on changing to become better and stronger employees."

"It will help future leaders with this Company get in touch with themselves, thus learning how to better communicate with others on the jobs, leading to more successful relationships."

"People will get a very good snapshot of who they are and ways to help these areas in a positive manner."

6. *How have you applied this learning to your personal life?*

As a result of the program, two participants quit smoking and several lost weight.

"I am much more attentive to the time and needs of my family."

"Increasing happiness in my life which led to less stress."

"It made me focus on character flaws in my personality that continue to hold me back."

"The course has made my personal relationships more valuable to me."

"I am more patient with my wife. I have become more in tune with her, and she has become more in tune with me."

"I have learned that I do not have to fix or to be right about everything. Sometimes, they just want you to listen."

"My wife is the biggest priority and it has made me take the time to reflect how I can improve our relationship and build on things for the future."

"Much of what I worked on was in my personal life. As I have developed ways to cope with my wife and stepson, this has eased much tension. This in turn has eased my overall happiness that has taught lessons at work."

"To be more in touch with my wife and family."

"Many of the exercises and tactics are transferable to home."

"Better, longer, and deeper discussions with my wife. I always try to look for good qualities in others."

"I work to show my spouse and kids that I really care by listening better and expressing feelings."

7. *How will you apply this learning going forward in your career? Do you think it will have a positive impact on your career? Explain.*

"I can only improve how others perceive me and promote positive feedback from those I have worked with. There is no better compliment to your management skills than when you hear, 'Can I be on your team?'"

"I believe that this course will advance my career beyond those who have not had this type of training."

"I will always work on ways to improve my emotional mind. It has shown me ways to help with stress and deal with different people and how to be a better me."

"I work with a very calm and fair man whom I wish to be more like. These tools I learned in this class will help to that end."

"To have a more one on one relationship with owners and subcontractors which will in turn create the trust and support from all. This has to have a positive impact."

"This can do nothing but help. If I am happier, more confident, and more self-assured, I will do a better job."

"The tools and ideas learned in the course will better prepare all of us for our roles as leaders."

"Managing the emotional side of our work reduces stress and allows me to enjoy the parts of construction that were often overlooked because I was too busy dealing with difficult people or fire drills."

"Not only will it help me, but I can use the lessons to mentor younger employees."

"I know now to put myself in other people's shoes before reacting, even if they're in the wrong. I also know that sometimes I have to stand firm and kick butt, too."

"I will continue to grow as a person and improve myself, which carries over into the way I handle myself on the jobsite."

"The course has given a positive impact. It helps us work on stronger relationships with clients."

"I truly know that it will have a positive impact on my career and my life."

"The insight will help me develop even better leadership traits. This will for sure help me with my career. The more leadership tools I can develop, the better leader I will become."

8. *What is the most important thing you have received from this program?*

"Tools for improvement."

"The ability to look within myself."

"The ability to know how I feel and how someone else feels ahead of time, then try to approach a situation the best way possible."

"I am more comfortable with who I am and what I want. That focus makes it easy to persistently pursue my goals."

"A better understanding of my strengths and weaknesses."

"Improved self-awareness, increased happiness, confidence, and optimism."

"Confidence in the fact that you really <u>can</u> teach an old dog new tricks."

"The positive effect that I have seen in myself and everyone in the class."

"Stress release and how to deal with it."

"Knowledge of how to be a better person and some tools to get there."

9. *Would you recommend this program to others at the Company? In other words, do you feel that this program has value to others at the Company? Why or why not?*

Everyone answered yes. Some comments:

"Great opportunity to learn some solid techniques and practices that make a difference in your 'whole' life."

"This class would help any individual learn how to communicate, manage, and lead with their heart <u>and</u> their head adding to genuine integrity of the Company."

"I will recommend this program to all of the operations personnel in my charge."

"You learn so much on how to manage yourself and how to be a better and more productive employee."

"Although I do not believe the EQi verse for verse, I do think it stimulates thoughts, concepts, and habits that are beneficial to individuals, team building, and the Company profit."

"I recommend to all managers and Superintendents to help deal with the stress that comes with our industry and improve all of your relationships."

"Top management that has not participated in this particular course and most other employees as well will benefit."

"I would specifically recommend it to field guys who are moving into superintendent roles who grew up in the trades."

"This program is not built for one type of person. It will work for all as long as you have an open mind and listen and be aware."

"I think it is a great program not only for the lessons learned,, but also for the new relationships created with people in the Company that you might not have otherwise met."

"It may not help everyone, but I feel anyone who makes a concerted effort to improve on this, then they will see benefits even if the effort is small. If someone attends and doesn't agree with the approach, they should be able to avoid or quit the class without it affecting them professionally."

"The program has definite value and should be continued.

It should be stressed to future classes to get involved with the process from the start. I was skeptical in the beginning, but after successful classes, I believe that new members should be involved earlier."

"It helps us all to be well rounded and can help us to work better together."

"This program is a good thing. I see others in day to day activities and think-if they would have taken this course, they wouldn't be acting or reacting the way they are. This is a course to polish skills."

10. *Do you have any other comments?*

"This training was very educational. Thanks for the training and the opportunity."

"Great program and hope other programs like this are offered in the future."

"I think this is a very helpful tool although a bit touchy-feely at times. It's probably getting out of that comfort zone is probably very effective."

"Short and sweet-this training was great and has impacted my life at work, home, and alone."

"I am privileged to be asked to take this course. I thought it was great for me and I learned a lot. I would take more if offered."

"Very good class. I hope anyone with five plus years should be forced to take it."

"I was surprised at the improvement I went through during the past eight months."

"Outstanding class. We need more of these classes which will help with our development. This will create a better employee by better emotional awareness and a less stressed employee."

Case Study 2
Summary Report for
Future Leaders 2005

Prepared by
G. Brent Darnell
Brent Darnell & Associates, Inc.

This is a report with results from a Future Leaders Program for the year 2005. The company elected to maintain anonymity because they believed that this work with emotional intelligence was a competitive advantage. The company is a top 100 general contractor. There were twenty-three program participants consisting of superintendents, assistant superintendents, project managers, assistant project managers, project engineers, one business developer, and one marketing person. The program ran from January to November 2005. The participants took the initial EQ-i® in January 2005. There were seven learning modules spread throughout the year consisting of the following:

1. EQ-Foundation for your Future
2. Teambuilding
3. Coaching and Mentoring
4. Stress Management/Time Management
5. Communication and Presentation
6. Negotiation Skills
7. Relationships and Creating Lifelong Learning

   Prior to the last learning module, the participants retook the EQ-i® and received individual feedback.

   Prior to the last learning module, the participants retook the EQ-i® and received individual feedback.

   Throughout the program, the participants received ongoing coaching and feedback a minimum of every three or four weeks via email and phone. This continuing dialogue between the participants and the coach allowed the group to stay focused on their goals and be accountable for their personal development plans.

EXECUTIVE SUMMARY:

Out of the twenty-six employees originally enrolled in the course, two participants left the company and one participant did not graduate due to a number of absences. The following data and quotes are from the remaining twenty-three participants.

Overall, according to the program participants, the program was beneficial. To the question, "Would you recommend this program to others?" everyone answered "Yes".

The results from the pre and post EQ-i® group scores (see next page) can be affected by many things-life changes, present job situations, career changes, and even the participants' state of mind when they took the evaluation. Although several of the participants decreased their EQ-i® scores, most increased their selected areas, and some increased dramatically.

The first thing we notice is that the group's total EQ increased by 6 (105.3 to 110.6), which means that they went from the average range to the high average range. Also, their interpersonal composite scale (empathy, social responsibility and interpersonal relationships) scores went up 5 points. Note the dramatic increases in the two lowest areas: emotional self-awareness (+7.5), interpersonal relationships (+8.9). Also, note the increase in stress tolerance (+6). There were also moderate increases in self-actualization (+3.9), empathy (+4.2), flexibility (+5), problem solving (+4.4), and happiness (+4.5). The great majority of these increases were statistically significant. 21

All other competencies increased by varying amounts. The group dramatically increased their scores in the areas where they

GROUP AVERAGES — BEFORE (■) & AFTER (■)

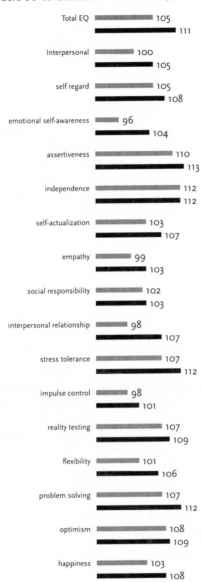

	Before	After
Total EQ	105	111
Interpersonal	100	105
self regard	105	108
emotional self-awareness	96	104
assertiveness	110	113
independence	112	112
self-actualization	103	107
empathy	99	103
social responsibility	102	103
interpersonal relationship	98	107
stress tolerance	107	112
impulse control	98	101
reality testing	107	109
flexibility	101	106
problem solving	107	112
optimism	108	109
happiness	103	108

previously had the lowest scores. This gave the group a much more balanced profile, which is usually desirable. The scores indicate that the group is much more aware of their own emotions, which is the first step toward good emotional management. They are also better at relationships and more empathetic toward others. The scores also indicate that they are more flexible, take a more systematic approach to solving problems, and are somewhat happier and self-satisfied than when they first took the EQ-i® in January of 2005 (self actualization and happiness increases). In addition, even though they still exhibit a crisis management style (high stress tolerance, low impulse control) they are better able to handle their stress (significant increase in stress tolerance).

FEEDBACK QUESTIONNAIRE SUMMARY:

We asked the participants to fill out a detailed questionnaire at the end of the program to gauge the overall effectiveness. Here is a summary of their answers:

1. *What have you learned about yourself during this course?*

"I have learned how easy it is to improve myself when I put my mind to it."

"That I can change. There were times when I felt like The Karate Kid ... why am I continuing to 'wax on, wax off?', but in the end, the lessons really paid off."

"Problems can be solved on your own with the proper tools."

"That what I thought worked doesn't necessarily work. There are different ways to achieve goals to make everyone happy instead of just taking a hard line approach."

"Think about how others see things and their thoughts, think about my thoughts and actions, still need to work on minimizing criticism."

2. *What specific strategies from your EQ workbook did you choose for your personal development plan?*

"The primary strategy I worked on was finding centering techniques. In addition, I worked on relaxation techniques that coordinated with the centering techniques. Secondly, I have made an effort to listen. Listening to others has given me a different perspective to deal with situations and people. Before, I think it was strictly reactionary."

"Meditation-helped me clear my mind. Exercise-more energy, reduced stress. Diet-more energy, generally feel better."

3. *What have you learned about others from this course?*

"That good relationships really affect the outcome of a project."

"You can create good relationships regardless of the differences as long as you can tap into others' values, interests, etc."

"I have seen several superintendents make great strides, and my understanding of their perceptions got better."

4. *What practical things have you learned from this course?*

"I have learned that doing even the simplest tasks can better prepare you for situations in day to day life. For example, making a list or checklist can cut down on impulsive decisions."

"I can now sense or feel when the pressure is getting great and the stress is mounting. My body acts in different ways and understanding these feelings is helping out during these busy times."

"I have learned some effective negotiation techniques. I have learned that how you say something is much more important than what you say."

"Keep your body hydrated at all times. Deep breathing at my desk for a few minutes helps me relax."

"How to meditate, how to make changes by specific actions."

"I talk more to my co-workers and ask more about how they feel."

"How to balance personal life with professional. How to recognize ways to improve relationships and where they can be fixed. How to recognize different personality traits and how to adapt myself to fit them."

"I am a better listener and much more patient."

"It is not what you know, but the way you present things. Leading and motivating is not just pointing and screaming."

5. *How have you applied this learning to your professional life?*

"I have applied it every day, making myself do things that continue to help me in my job and being successful."

"Leaving [a bad] situation, even briefly, has allowed me to not act in anger or impulsively."

"Listening, not reacting, has led to a more positive approach to my professional life."

"By spending more time listening to what people want. By remaining calm during the storm to be the voice of reason."

"I have tried to step back and put myself in my co-worker's shoes before making assumptions."

"I have learned to build a relationship, coach and motivate those that may need some training in lieu of just 'finding a better fit.'"

6. *Do you think these types of courses will help the company's business? If so, how?*

Everyone answered in the affirmative. Some specific comments:

"Absolutely. If everyone can improve like I have and take away what I have from this class, we will be a better company."

"No doubt about it. This course has changed my management style."

"I think relationships are very important in the construction business and good relationships with clients mean repeat business and good relationships with subcontractors mean successful projects."

"Yes, it gives us skills to better communicate."

"These types of courses will greatly benefit our leadership. If lessons learned in courses such as this are passed along, our leadership should have more successful projects."

"YES!! Relationships and impressions are just as important as bricks and mortar."

"Yes I do. Once I took the EQ-i®, I saw where I needed to improve. Years of construction on the jobsite and you can get into a rut. This helped me change some things such as how I work with my subs."

"EQ development can improve daily tasks and their effectiveness and success."

"Yes. By making our managers more well-rounded and more focused on the relationship aspect of our business, which is becoming increasingly important."

"Yes. This course helps improve interpersonal skills which are key in developing relationships with colleagues, subcontractors, and owners."

"Absolutely. Particularly the field guys. Everyone could use it, but I see bigger improvements on the field side."

"Yes – it gives people goals, aspirations, and methods that not only are designed to assist in the professional world, but enrich their personal lives at the same time."

"Provide leadership skills to their employees that will help retain people."

"I already see a change in upper management. If we as the next class change we should see a trickle-down effect."

"Yes. Understanding why you or others behave the way they do is a definite competitive advantage."

"Every company has smart, knowledgeable people. It's the relationship and trust that someone has in you that makes the difference."

7. *How have you applied this learning to your personal life?*

"A lot has changed recently in my personal life and I have used the emotional self-awareness improvement to help me understand how to deal with the issue and move on, as I understand how I truly feel about it."

"The course has truly helped at home. I am more understanding, but need to continue to develop."

"My focus on family and happiness is important to me, and that balance between work and play will help me be more successful."

"Will continue to examine my self-awareness and try different relaxation techniques at home."

"I have taken more quality time with my family, which has led to more personal enrichment."

"I listen to my wife more. We talk a lot more. We try to do more things together, take more time off from work, and take my vacation."

"My relationship with my wife and kids is better as I can put myself in their position."

"I have applied all of these in my marriage as well as outside of it. I am taking the time to sit and listen more to my wife and make time for both of us. I also take the time to make my expectations more clear to others."

"I have tried to understand my parents more, and it has helped in my relationship with my wife as well."

"Taken more time to devote to my family. Tried to be more appreciative of my wife and understand her and adversities in her role as a home maker."

"I am trying things that I never would have tried previously."

"My wife and I are seeing benefits from the course. We are working on our time management by setting up a schedule at home. We have a daughter who has ADHD, and this seems to be helping out with her as well."

8. *How will you apply this learning in your future career? Do you think it will have a positive impact? Explain.*

"I will promote the things that have been helpful to me to others I train. I will try and make others aware of how doing the little things can make a big difference in personal and in work life."

"Absolutely. This course has been something I've really needed. It has helped my relationships, with clients, co-workers, and at home."

"I will discuss my goals with my supervisor and push ahead to meet them."

"I have already learned that the calmer I am, the better the team works."

"I believe it has already had a significant impact on my career. Since the beginning of the course, I have changed projects, and with the modifications made, it is easier and more fulfilling. Employing techniques I learned has led to better relationships."

"It will help me deal with people in a better way. Yes, I think it will have a positive impact on my career and as a person."

"It will impact my career positively because it already has."

"As I continue to manage more people than actual work, these skills are vital to my understanding of how to motivate team members."

"Yes, it has given me an organized approach to defining my goals. Once you know your goals, you can develop a plan to get there."

9. What is the most important thing you have gained from this program?

"I have found a new understanding of myself, and I have learned more about how my mind works. I have found some of my weaknesses and continue to work on improving them."

"Empathy, confidence, patience . . . most importantly, it has made me aware."

"I have learned more about my own personality and what potential obstacles stand in my way of success. I feel I have the tools to overcome them."

"That stress does make a difference in how I behave/perform and that it affects others."

"That I needed to change and that if I change, things will be better."

"The understanding that I am in control of my feelings and emotions. I will succeed or fail determined by how I carry myself."

"How to feel good about myself and be more confident."

"The knowledge that the company feels that a well-rounded and developed employee is preferred brings [me] comfort. This knowledge is in addition to the many tools learned during this process."

"Understanding of why so many field guys don't understand Project Managers and vice versa."

"Awareness, implementation, and measuring results."

"Better life balance."

"Confidence."

"Opened my eyes to improvements that I need to make in relationships with people."

"An eye-opening view at certain areas of my life-my motivations and expectations. How I am perceived by others."

"Becoming more aware of what is happening around me."

10. *Would you recommend this program to others? In other words, do you feel that this program has value to others? Why or why not?*
Every participant said that they would recommend this program to others because they felt that it would benefit them and make the company better. Some comments:

"Yes. I would like to see certain "construction" cultures change."

"I believe this program has significant value to all leadership positions. Becoming more effective leaders enhances our relationships and will inherently aid our business position."

"I would recommend this program without reservation. The areas available for improvement and growth are untouched in other training."

"I think that anyone could benefit from this course."

"This class has value for anyone in this company. Learning the impact of emotions in personal and professional situations is key for a successful individual and company."

"Yes. It has helped me gain perspective and improve my skills. I feel better about who I am and where I am going."

"Yes. I believe this program and its results (look at the number of promotions) demonstrate how valuable this course can be to individuals as they progress through their career and to the company as a whole."

"This program forces you to take a look at yourself, pick out developmental needs, and work on them. It makes you a better human being."

11. *Has your position changed during this course? If yes, how has this course helped you with your new position?*
Eleven out of twenty-three employees in the course were promoted. Here are some of the comments:

"My improvement has helped my in my [new] position as you can see by my improved performance."

"Skills and techniques learned have assisted me with my new duties and responsibilities."

"The course has helped me enhance those skills which helped me get the promotion."

"Yes. I hope that as a manager of a team this course helps me know my strengths and weaknesses so that I can work to improve these and lead the team by example."

"I have newfound confidence that I am making informed decisions."

12. *Do you have any other comments?*

"Thanks for the help with improving myself. It has helped me personally and professionally."

"I was apprehensive about this type of training in the beginning. However, after completing the course, and visualizing my own personal growth on the EQ-i®s, I realize that the effort given has netted significant results."

"Great class!! I have made noticeable changes in my life."

"I am extremely grateful for the opportunity to participate in this course. Not only did I grow as a leader both personally and professionally, I made some new friends and strengthened some relationships that already existed."

Summary Report for
Leadership Development Program 2005–2006
Note: This is an anonymous report at the request of the company.

Prepared by
G. Brent Darnell
Brent Darnell & Associates, Inc.

This is a report with results from a Management Development Program for the year 2005–2006. The company elected to maintain anonymity because they believed that this emotional intelligence program was a competitive advantage. The company is a multi-national holding company for a group of manufacturers/retailers/installers/service companies. This company is closely related to the construction industry. There were seventeen program participants from various parts of this industry, sales, production, customer service, training, and human resources. The participants were from The UK, The Netherlands, Finland, Sweden, Norway, Denmark, Germany, Austria, and Spain. The program ran from March 2005 to February 2006. The participants took the initial EQ-i® in March 2005. During the first week, the Personal Leadership week, the following learning modules were covered:

1. EQ-Foundation for your Future –
   creation of development plans
2. Cultural basics
3. Coaching and Mentoring
4. Introduction to Yoga
5. Building and Leading Teams
6. Coaching, Motivating, Mentoring
7. Stress Management

8. Time Management/Life Balance
9. Creating and Maintaining Relationships

The second week focused on business strategy, which included business simulations and modules on strategic thinking. During this week, the participants revisited their EQ development plans and gave the group an update. They also discussed barriers to achieving their goals and strategies for development that were effective.

The third week was finance and business development. The focus was on technical skills, but the participants updated the group again on their EQ development progress.

The fourth and final week was titled Management of Change. The final session of this final week focused on how to create lifelong learning. Prior to the final session, the participants re-took the EQ-i® and received individual feedback.

Throughout the program, the participants received ongoing coaching and feedback every three or four weeks via email and phone conferences. This continuing dialogue between the participants and the coach encouraged the group to stay focused on their goals and be accountable for their personal development plans.

EXECUTIVE SUMMARY:

Out of the twenty employees originally enrolled in the course, three participants left The Company. The following data and quotes are from the remaining seventeen participants.

Everyone in the program felt that the program was beneficial. To the question, "Would you recommend this program to others?" everyone answered "Yes".

The results from the EQ-i® group scores (see below) can be affected by many things-life changes, present job situations, career changes, and even the participants' state of mind when they took the evaluation. Most participants increased their EQ-i® scores and some increased dramatically. Even the participants who decreased their scores used the second evaluation as an opportunity to develop more awareness and understanding of their strengths and weaknesses.

One of the participants decided to work on her social responsibility, which was relatively low. Eleven months later, at the end of the program, when she took the EQ-i® again, she found that her social responsibility score was even lower. Interestingly enough, her self-actualization, happiness, and optimism had increased dramatically. When we discussed these numbers, I asked her why she chose to work on social responsibility. She told me that she believed that it was the right thing to do, that she thought her family and friends wanted her to spend more time with them. I asked her if she had spent more time with family and friends in an effort to increase her social responsibility. She replied that she had not. She told me that work was particularly hectic, and she had been working non-stop since the beginning of the program. She mostly worked alone and not in groups or teams. She also told me that she felt a little guilty for working so much.

I asked her if she enjoyed working and she replied that it was the most important thing in her life. She said that she loved the challenge and felt that the company needed her during this particularly difficult period. It made her feel valued and important. That was the reason for her significant increases in self-actualization, happiness, and optimism. I suggested that perhaps this second evaluation revealed that during this period in her life, her work, which gives her great joy, is something that she would do well to focus on. In addition, since she worked alone, this way of working did not contribute to increasing her social responsibility. This conversation was a great relief to her. Perhaps all she needed was permission to enjoy her work life without the guilt. So, in this case, although the competency she was working on decreased, the results of the second EQ-i® gave us some real insights into her personal and professional life.

The first thing we notice is that the group's total EQ increased by 6 (104 to 110), which means that they went from the average range to the high average range. Also, their interpersonal composite scale (empathy, social responsibility and interpersonal relationships) scores went up 7 points, and is approaching the high average range. Note the dramatic increases in several areas: emotional self-awareness (+11), empathy (+7), interpersonal relationships (+7), self-actualization (+6), and happiness (+6). There were also moderate increases that indicate behavioral shifts in self-regard (+5), assertiveness (+5), and social responsibility (+5). The great majority of these increases were statistically significant. 22

All other competencies increased by varying amounts. These shifts and increases gave the group a much more balanced profile, which is usually desirable. The scores indicate that the group is much more aware of their own emotions (increased emotional self-awareness), which is the first step toward good emotional management. They are also better at relationships (increased interpersonal relationship skills) and more empathetic toward others (increased empathy). They will tend to work better in a group or team setting (increased social responsibility). The scores also indicate that they are generally happier with their lives and feel better about themselves than when they took the first EQ-i® in March/April of 2005 (increases in self-actualization and happiness). In addition, they are able to assert themselves better (increased assertiveness). The group scores indicate that they still live in a world of chaos (high stress tolerance and relatively low impulse control). It is recommended that The Company focus on stress management and time management skills in order to help with this issue and avoid stress related symptoms such as illness and burnout.

GROUP AVERAGES — BEFORE (■) & AFTER (■)

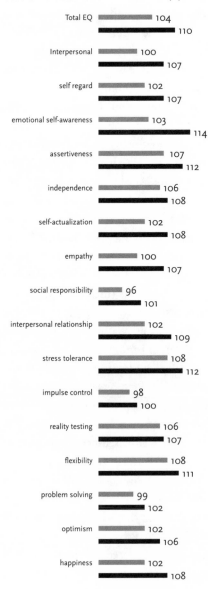

	Before	After
Total EQ	104	110
Interpersonal	100	107
self regard	102	107
emotional self-awareness	103	114
assertiveness	107	112
independence	106	108
self-actualization	102	108
empathy	100	107
social responsibility	96	101
interpersonal relationship	102	109
stress tolerance	108	112
impulse control	98	100
reality testing	106	107
flexibility	108	111
problem solving	99	102
optimism	102	106
happiness	102	108

We asked the participants to fill out a detailed questionnaire at the end of the program to gauge the overall effectiveness. Here is a summary of their answers.

1. *What have you learned about yourself during this course?*

"I discovered that I did not spend enough time listening to others or having what I would previously have deemed 'unproductive' social conversations at work. I have since recognized that, in moderation, these interactions form the basis of strong relationships with colleagues, something that is needed to be successful and happy at work."

"I have relearned that it is important for me to practice some form of sports as a balance against stress. Also, the meditation sessions help me with my daily stress. My family support helps me to have good balance between my job and my private life. "

"I realize the importance of a well-balanced life and the importance of time and stress management. I also realize that I have to show more interest in others, help them if necessary, listen better, be more open, and show my feelings more."

"It has been a very interesting journey. I learned a lot about myself and the massive palette of tools and methods we can use to adopt, adapt, and improve. I also learned that it is possible to change in both behavior and attitude towards other people and solve problems if you put your mind to it. I learned that stress is a major player in how well you function in your work and in your private life, and that you have to act and do something about it before it gets too much power over your skills and ability."

"The course has made me stop and think about my career and what I want to get out of the next five years. The course will help me challenge myself more than I would have previously."

"Quite a lot. During the courses I have learned that I am in a position to develop myself constantly if I am focusing on the right things."

"I learned that I am too structured and need to stop sweating the small stuff. I have learned to relax and not be so serious."

2. *What practical things have you learned from this course?*

"The meditation was great."

"The interaction between people is so important, and I try to practice it with more energy in my team and also in the company."

"I handle stressful situations much better than before this course, and I realize the importance of recovery time in order to be more effective in business and private life."

"I feel that my personal toolbox is fresh and loaded with new stuff. I found a lot of ways to work on myself and have learned methods to deal with people and management teams. Sports, yoga, and meditation are also a part of the agenda! Who would believe that it could happen to an IT-freak!"

"Meditation and relaxation techniques. When considering strategy, establish visions and goals. Feeling fit and healthy creates more optimism."

3. *How have you applied that learning to your day-to-day professional life?*

"I think that everyone can see that I have changed in my behavior. I try to put as much of my new learning in action in the daily work and with a much more balanced attitude with less stress. I am more happy with me."

"The course has increased my awareness of how people perceive me, and it is important that I build in a self-check system which ensures that I continually remind myself of this. In addition to this, I am more critical as to how I prioritize my time."

"In many ways. Now I am much more aware about how important it is to listen in order to make the right decisions."

"Meditation. I try to use this now and then during my working day."

"I take a more strategic approach. It is important to understand who the stakeholders are and, more importantly the blockers, when trying to sell an idea. Controlling my 'temptation to act' has made a big difference to my professional and personal life."

4. *Do you think these types of courses will help The Company's business? If so, how?*

"Yes of course. The content of the course was extremely relevant and well delivered; if everyone got as much from it as I have then it can't help but improve strategic ability, leadership, and action within the business. It helps to build relationships between businesses also."

"Of course! Being part of the course is a reward in itself and it gives you motivation."

"My personal opinion is that The Company`s business will [be] helped a lot. The networking is very important and it builds trusting relationships."

"Definitely. One thing is the course itself, but I think that the relationships in the group and the knowledge you get from other units in The Company is the most important thing."

"In the past as well as today you very often see people being promoted to managers because they are very good specialists, but they don't have management skills. I really thing this kind of course will help The Company's business. It is important to develop the management skills when leading and working with employees."

5. How have you applied this learning to your personal life?

"The EQ was a help during a very tough period in my life."

"I learned a lot about my personal life. I learned to listen more and to be more sensitive and understanding. But I learned also to say no if necessary."

"I take more responsibility for others, try to understand their feelings, and try to help if people want my help. I also realize that I feel much better when I talk about my feelings (or show them) with good friends – not solving everything by myself. I did not do this before this course."

"I take more time off to do things I like: cooking, sports, friends, and spending time with my wife. I see the importance in having a happy, well-balanced life."

"My wife thinks I listen more and that I am more flexible. I feel even more confident than before, and others notice it as well."

"In my personal life I try to be more aware of my needs than I was before."

"I have increased my focus on better balance between my work and private life. I also try to be more present in the moment in my private life."

"Yes, and I feel that I am a better person for it. I spend more time with my children, find it easier to interact with friends and make new friends."

6. How will you apply this learning as you move forward in your career? Do you think it will have a positive impact on your career? Explain.

"I hope it will have a positive impact. I am making a career plan rather than just sitting back and letting things happen. This will make me a happier person as well as a successful one. I think I have a better understanding of business and leadership and hope that this will be apparent to others who could be influential in the achievement of my career goals."

"Most of all, it is important that you sometimes stop to reflect on yourself, something that you were forced to do during this course. I will try to use this knowledge to keep learning."

"I think a lot of things which I learned during this course will be applied without thinking about it consciously."

"I am 100% certain that this learning will have a positive impact on my career."

"This learning has become a cornerstone for my personal and professional career. I am *convinced* that this is a positive and helpful tool, which gives power, encouragement, commitment, and self-confidence."

"I use it every day. I feel that I have greatly increased the development of my business and personal skills."

"It has already had a positive impact on my career."

"Applying the theory is one thing, but the key to success is how I personally interact and manage the project teams."

7. *What is the most important thing you have gained from this program?*

"More confidence in myself."

"A better understanding of my strengths and weaknesses EQ-wise!"

"The most important thing that I improved is my emotional skills."

"The importance of a well-balanced life for my business and my private life."

"As a direct result of the learning from the course, I spend more time reflecting and analyzing my performance and approach than I used to. This is helping me to understand how I am perceived by others and how I can use this to influence situations."

"I have learned that there is no problem that cannot be solved. Sometimes it's good to make a step back to get an overview!"

"The whole EQ-i® made me sit back and look at myself. It helped me to understand where I was weak (impulse control, social responsibility) and gave me the tools to improve. I believe I am much more approachable now, a lot more empathetic, and I am able to communicate with others better."

"The program has given me the confidence to enjoy my current work and to develop future strategy."

8. *Would you recommend this program to others at The Company? In other words, do you feel that this program has value to others at The Company? Why or why not?*

Every participant said that they would recommend this program to others at The Company because they felt that it would benefit them and make The Company better.

"Yes, it has value! I recommended to my CEO that he consider sending other members of the senior management team. It would increase the strategic capability within our business and promote effective leadership that could then cascade down to other managers."

"Definitely! I have already recommended it to a colleague that I hope will participate next year."

"It should be obligatory to join these courses if you are a part of the management team."

"I would not hesitate to recommend the course to others."

"I already have. One of my colleagues is participating in the next program."

"Yes, I recommended it already to lots of people in our business unit because I know that to be successful, people must understand that lifelong learning is so important. They have to get the skills to handle stress and improve themselves."

9. *Do you have any other comments?*

"The course has broadened my thinking, and I am grateful that I had the opportunity to take part in it."

"It has been a fantastic experience and one that I would not hesitate to do again if the opportunity arose."

"The program was excellent."

"I am very satisfied with this program."

"I was very apprehensive and intimidated when first asked to attend the development program. However, the group of delegates in the program and the facilitators have all been excellent, and the training has been first class! I would never have believed that I could benefit from meditation, relaxation, and applying other specifics relating to a personal development plan. It has certainly made me a better person inside and outside of work. Many thanks!"

CASE STUDY 4

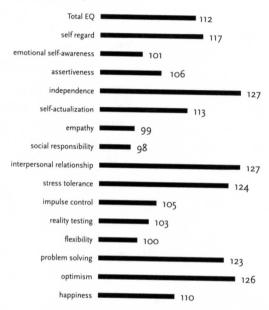

A forty-seven year old construction worker with a high school education became a successful building contractor. His EQ-i® results, which are shown above, may explain why he has done so well.

This person's total EQ score is close to the upper limits of the average range (112), which suggests that he is well prepared to deal with the usual demands and pressures of everyday life. By studying six of his highest scores, it became quite clear as to how he became so successful in his present occupation. His intrapersonal strength stems from his positive self-regard (SR=117) and a very high degree of independence (IN=127). Moreover, one of his highest scores is in the interpersonal relationship domain (IR=127). These intrapersonal and interpersonal strengths combine with a very high degree of optimism (OP=126), stress tolerance (ST=124), and a down-to-earth, highly developed ability to solve problems (PS=123).

Other people consider him to be a "very good person to work with and for." Interestingly, he received a total IQ score of 102 on an intelligence test that was given toward the end of his last year in high school. An IQ of 102 places his cognitive intelligence in the middle of the average range; and his grades in high school were also average.

Case Study 5
Predicting Professional Failure
in the Corporate World

CASE STUDY 5

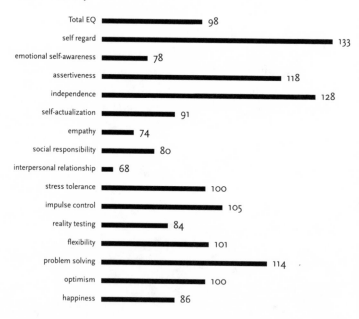

A 30-year-old financial consultant was dismissed by a number of companies for unsuccessful performance in the workplace. Five years earlier, she had graduated at the top of her class in a doctoral program at a prestigious Ivy League business school. In interviews, she came across as very articulate, intelligent, and sure of herself. After presenting a number of very complimentary letters of recommendation from her graduate school, making an excellent impression when interviewed, and receiving an "Extraverted Feeling with Introverted Sensing" personality type (ESFJ) on the Myers-Briggs Type Indicator (Myers & Mc-

Caulley, 1985), this woman was hired as a financial consultant by one of New England's oldest and most reputable investment companies. However, after creating a situation that resulted in a well-publicized lawsuit, which nearly caused serious financial damage to the company, she was asked to leave her position.

Afterwards, it became clear as to why she had been unable to keep a job for more than a year since leaving graduate school – a fact that was somehow overlooked when she was first considered for the position. Shortly after being hired, she and a randomly selected group of people at work volunteered for a study, which examined the connection between cognitive and emotional intelligence. As a part of this study, she was given the Wechsler Adult Intelligence Scale (WAIS; Wechsler, 1939) and the Bar-On EQ-i®. While she received a very high total IQ score of 138, she received a total EQ score of 96. Her EQ-i® results appear above. An in-depth evaluation of her EQ profile sheds a great deal of light on her professional instability and lack of business success.

Based on the nature of the validity scores (PI=122), she probably attempted to give a very positive impression of herself, while de-emphasizing her negative qualities; the very high Self-Regard score (SR=133) supports this assumption. This constellation, together with a very low emotional self-awareness score (ES=78), could possibly mean that she is not aware of her feelings or self in general. A very high Independence score (IN=128) and very low Interpersonal Relationship score (IR=68) suggest that she is a loner, perhaps due to a serious inability to relate to others. Moreover, her difficulty in empathizing with others (EM=74) contributes to her struggle to relate to people and to feel part of the larger social context (RE=80).

Case Study 6
Caddell Construction Company:
Case Study of a Project Team

Prepared by
G. Brent Darnell
January 2005

INTRODUCTION This program started with a phone call from
Monte McKinney, the Vice President of Building Operations
for Caddell Construction Company, a top 200 contractor in
the United States. He asked if we thought that emotional intelligence would help one of his project teams at the Barracks and
Operations Complex at Fort Bragg, North Carolina. Monte was
looking for a way to improve their interpersonal skills and make
them more effective. There were several personality conflicts
with the Corps of Engineers, the owners on the project. The
Corps of Engineers has a reputation for being a very demanding
and tough client. Our belief was that by increasing the project
team's emotional intelligence, it would improve their leadership
effectiveness, which, in turn, would positively impact individual
and organizational performance.

Five members of the Caddell project team took the EQ-i® and
participated in a half-day session on April 16, 2004, where they
implemented individual EQ development plans. Between April
and December of 2004, they received emails and phone calls
from Brent Darnell to assess progress and coach them through
their development plans and any difficulties or questions. As the
graph below indicates, the quantitative data shows amazing differences between emotional intelligence scores between April and
December of 2004. The qualitative analysis shows the personal
impact the training had on the participants, both at home and

at work. The participants with the lowest pre-training scores demonstrated the highest increase in their EQ-i®s.

QUALITATIVE RESULTS   Participants have reported that the emotional intelligence training has produced direct and positive impacts in such areas as:

RELATIONSHIPS AND SOCIAL SKILLS "I try to listen to others, and develop a sense of how they feel before trying to impose my feelings on them. I feel I have definitely increased my social skills in the past several months, and with a recently updated job description, I was forced to become more independent on the jobsite, nearly overnight."

STRESS MANAGEMENT "I have begun a lifestyle management health program at the local health club. I started in February 2004 and have continued until the present. I have lost about fifteen pounds and increased my strength tremendously. I feel a lot better physically and emotionally."

IMPULSE CONTROL "The best help for me is to not act on something immediately when a problem surfaces, but rather take a breath and then deal with the problem after the initial reaction period is over."

CONFLICT RESOLUTION "When faced with a conflict or difference of opinion, I've first been very conscientious of letting others speak their mind entirely, while concentrating on understanding their position and feelings. Then I have worked towards explaining my position, by expressing my thoughts and feelings and trying to get them to understand my perspective. Following this, I've pushed for a mutual understanding, and agreement, by presenting solutions, and being fair and optimistic. For the most part, this approach has produced positive outcomes, and I feel that by continuing to use this approach in difficult situations, I will improve and become more successful in resolving conflicts."

GROUP AVERAGES — BEFORE (■) & AFTER (■)

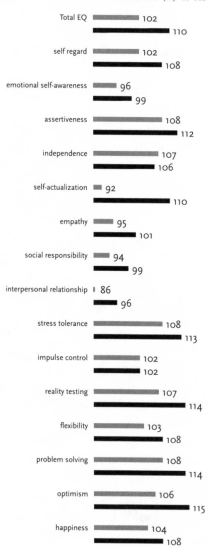

	Before	After
Total EQ	102	110
self regard	102	108
emotional self-awareness	96	99
assertiveness	108	112
independence	107	106
self-actualization	92	110
empathy	95	101
social responsibility	94	99
interpersonal relationship	86	96
stress tolerance	108	113
impulse control	102	102
reality testing	107	114
flexibility	103	108
problem solving	108	114
optimism	106	115
happiness	104	108

See the graph on the previous page for the before and after EQ-i® scores. The participants increased their scores in most areas, but several areas were significant, including: Self-actualization, interpersonal relationships, and optimism

These increased scores in key areas tell us that the team has greater self-confidence and are happier and more optimistic. They have become more adept at handling interpersonal relationships as well, which has resulted in a more effective work environment with clients and peers.

What the data doesn't reveal are the un-measurable outcomes of the program. This group was very cohesive and even in the early stages, began to use each other as resources. Per one participant: "We talk about EQ at least once a month if not more."

CONCLUSION Overall, the participants were very satisfied with the emotional intelligence training program.

"All in all, I think the emotional intelligence education I received from you is very helpful in my life and work".

"Thanks for your help. I will recommend that others can benefit from this experience if they are open to self-analysis and change."

The results speak for themselves. This team increased their effectiveness dramatically. As incredible as these results were, they were achieved with a single training session and remote, follow-up coaching. Imagine what the results would be if we had delivered more learning modules that addressed the specific developmental needs of the group. These types of programs are radically different from event based, informational training programs. With an emotional intelligence program, you truly can create positive, fundamental change within the individual. This, in turn, will create fundamental change within the organization.

Case Study 7
Outcome Study of a Leadership Development
Assessment and Training Program
Based on Emotional Intelligence

STUDY AUTHORS:

Margareta Sjölund, Ph.D from Kandidata in Sweden (www. kandidata.se) and Henrik Gustafsson, Psychologist

EMOTIONAL INTELLIGENCE CONSULTANT:

Kate Cannon, M.Ed.

PROGRAM DIRECTOR: G. Brent Darnell

PROGRAM NAME: SMP 5

DATE: September 2001

EXECUTIVE SUMMARY:

In making the decision to incorporate emotional intelligence training into a management development program for a large, multi – national contractor (top 5 in the United States) referred to in this study as "S", the stakeholders held the hypothesis that being emotionally intelligent positively impacts leadership effectiveness and that leadership effectiveness, in turn, has a positive impact on individual and organizational performance.

The analysis of the participants' pre and post scores revealed positive and significant improvements in their emotional intelligence as measured by the EQ-i®. The participants with the lowest pre-training scores demonstrated the highest increase in their EQ-i®s, demonstrating the value of the program especially for low performers.

The anecdotal examples the participants provided offer support for the positive impact the program is having on performance. Further, they consistently report improvements in other areas of their lives, e.g. personal relationships.

As one participant summed it up, "Emotional intelligence is in my view a very extensive and important aspect of both professional and private life. It has made me more aware of, and has given me a different perspective, on these things. I now feel that SMP has given me tools for becoming more emotionally intelligent and hence, a better leader." He later concludes by saying, "Even though emotional intelligence training is not an entirely comfortable experience, this part of the program has been worth the effort."

The final data and the anecdotal reports reveal that the emotional intelligence training that was part of SMP 5 delivered the desired outcomes. The time period during which the training occurred was a time of unprecedented change for the company, changes the participants were required to both lead and cope with themselves.

Participants have reported that using the emotional intelligence training has produced direct and positive impacts in such areas as:

NEGOTIATIONS "I've learned that being able to understand what is motivating the other parties is essential for achieving your objectives."

MOTIVATING EMPLOYEES "… through listening and observation I have become more aware of employees' needs and concerns."

STRESS MANAGEMENT "I have increased the balance in life, which has increased my efficiency at work." Another perspective: "The knowledge of why I feel like I do in different situations helps to overcome daily problems."

MANAGING CHANGE AND COPING WITH CHANGE "When moving to a new job (in a new country) I needed to … make people feel comfortable in telling me the truth. There were a lot of problems and improvement areas, which needed to be identified. By using emotional intelligence, I think I got a good response, and I could, therefore, take quick action in creating a new structure."

COMMUNICATION   "My interpersonal interactions with customers, colleagues and subordinates have improved by being able to establish a deeper communication."

PRODUCTIVITY   "Proper listening and understanding have contributed to generating trust and therefore, more business opportunities." And from someone else, "Recovering focus leads to accurate analysis and proper decisions which have a direct impact on the bottom line."

CONFLICT RESOLUTION   "Listening and understanding others' problems and solving them so that both the individual and the company are winners is the most typical challenge in applying emotional intelligence."

What the data doesn't reveal are the un-measurable outcomes of the program. This group was very cohesive, and early on they began to use each other as resources. Certain training activities encouraged this behavior, but it was the "off-line" activity that will probably be one of the most beneficial results of this program. For example, when one participant was beginning to move to a new position, an emerging foreign market, he remembered that another participant had worked there before. So, he called him, asked for advice, and received useful information and resources. By their own admission, participating in SMP 5 has made the participants smarter about all parts of the company, more sensitive to other cultures, and more collaborative.

RESULTS Pre- and post-assessments show a significant increase in emotional intelligence for the great majority of participants. Please see the chart on the next page.

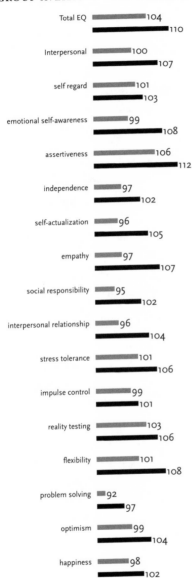

Total EQ 104 / 110

Interpersonal 100 / 107

self regard 101 / 103

emotional self-awareness 99 / 108

assertiveness 106 / 112

independence 97 / 102

self-actualization 96 / 105

empathy 97 / 107

social responsibility 95 / 102

interpersonal relationship 96 / 104

stress tolerance 101 / 106

impulse control 99 / 101

reality testing 103 / 106

flexibility 101 / 108

problem solving 92 / 97

optimism 99 / 104

happiness 98 / 102

CASE STUDIES

QUALITATIVE ANALYSIS "I think the knowledge and insight I got from the emotional intelligence package is one of a few really strong courses I ever attended in any company course so far."

After the second assessment, the participants were asked to answer three questions in order to provide additional insight into the impact of the program. Eighteen people responded to the request in time for the results to be a part of this report.

These questions were:

1. What external changes have you made in the last year?
2. Give some examples of how you dealt with this change.
3. Give some examples of situations where you used your skills and knowledge in emotional intelligence, and the outcome of the situation.

1. What external changes have you made in the last year?

On the first question, a majority (14) of the participants said that they had experienced a direct, major change over the past year. Most had been promoted or had been given additional responsibilities. Several had made significant geographical moves, some to new countries and/or other divisions of the company.

2. Give some examples of how you dealt with this change.

Several of the participants said that they had dealt with change through discussions with their managers or co-workers. The importance of goal setting, listening, and being open-minded were emphasized. Some of the respondents had delegated responsibility, and others had tried to implement changes step-by-step, in conjunction with realistic planning. Many reported on the large amount of stress they were dealing with, as well as the stress levels of their families and their employees.

3. Give some examples of situations where you used your skills and knowledge in emotional intelligence, and describe the outcome of the situation.

The majority of the respondents said that they had used their skills and knowledge in the context of relationships with other people, e.g. customers, co-workers, employees. Many participants spoke about their increased ability to handle difficult situations, e.g. letting people go as a result of organizational change.

Other respondents said that they had used the new skills to better understand what motivates other people and what their needs were. They have become better listeners, leading to constructive conflict resolution. As one person put it: "I have changed the way in which I deal with clients and owners, showing more of a respectful attitude to them, presenting myself to be more moderate, more aware of social responsibility."

CONCLUSION   Overall, the participants were very satisfied with the emotional intelligence aspect of the training program. (There was one exception.) When asked whether they would recommend the program to other leaders, 100% said yes. Typically, their reasons were such things as "It makes you a better leader," and "This is absolutely fundamental for success in the future."

A few more qualitative remarks: "It is perhaps difficult to point out specific situations where emotional intelligence training has proved effective, but it certainly addresses almost all aspects of dealing with people as a leader, such as motivation, giving constructive feedback (positive as well as negative), seeing possibilities in difficult challenges, etc."

"Deep impact! Showed me how to dig into my emotions rather than hide them behind a façade. Showed the importance of inter-relationships and the need to look over things with the heart … I feel stronger, less afraid to face changes, more excited for challenges. And even if I, myself, wouldn't have been able to recognize the deep impact of EQ, my family surely has. They do not stop telling me now how our entire relationship has grown. The same occurs with my work colleagues, who notice the change in excitement."

THE PEOPLE-PROFIT CONNECTION

Notes

1. *How to Win Friends and Influence People* by Dale Carnegie, Simon and Schuster Pocket Books, 1936.

2. *Emotional Intelligence* by Daniel Goleman, Bantam Books, 1995.

3. *"Comment on R.J. Emmerling and Daniel Goleman, Emotional Intelligence: Issues and Common Misunderstandings"* by David Caruso, PhD.

4. Source: National Institute for Occupational Safety and Health.

5. *Working with Emotional Intelligence* by Daniel Goleman, Bantam Books, 1998.

6. Source: *World Almanac*, 2004.

7. *Work to Live: The Guide to Getting a Life* by Joe Robinson, The Berkley Publishing Group, 2003.

8. *Engineering News Record*, July 19, 2004.

9. *"Coaching the Alpha Male"* by Kate Ludeman and Eddie Erlandson, Harvard Business Review, May2004.

10. *"Primal Leadership"* by Daniel Goleman, Richard Boyatziz, and Annie McKee, Harvard Business Review, December 2001.

11. *Joe Torre's Ground Rules for Winners* by Joe Torre with Henry Dreher, Hyperion, 1999.

12. *The Jobs Rated Almanac* by Les Krantz, St. Martin's Press, 2005.

13. Baby Boomers are born between 1946 and 1964. Generation X are born between 1965 and 1980. Generation Y are born between 1981 and 1999.

14. Percentages of women's positions courtesy of NAWIC (National Association of Women in Construction)

15. Source: FMI 2004–2005 Contractor Productivity Survey.

16. Source: National Academy of Sciences Task Force on Intellectual Property Management, September 1999.

17. Source: Annie R. Pearce, PhD., Program Director, Sustainable Facilties and Infrastructure Program, Georgia Institute of Technology, Atlanta, Georgia, USA.

18. Marilyn Elias, *"Sunlight Reduces Need for Pain Medication",* USA Today (March 2, 2004)

19. *"Drain on the Bottom Line",* Engineering News Record, May 8, 2006.

20. *Working with Emotional Intelligence* by Daniel Goleman, Bantam Books, 1998.

21. Multi-Health Systems conducted the data analysis and found that 12 pre-test to post-test differences were statistically significant.

22. Multi-Health Systems conducted the data analysis and found that 15 pre-test to post-test differences were statistically significant.

Biography & Contact Information

Brent Darnell is a leading authority on emotional intelligence and is a pioneer of its use in the construction industry. Brent has helped to improve the social competence of thousands of people working with over 70 companies in more than 15 countries around the world. There is constant demand for him to deliver speeches and train others using his comprehensive and unique approach that leads to lasting behavioral transformation. An engineer, author, actor, playwright and musician, Darnell gives presentations that are insightful, perceptive and wildly entertaining. The construction industry has embraced his work, and many top companies like Clark, Hardin, McCarthy, Heery, Centex, Caddell, and Skanska, have utilized his methods for their managers. He has also worked with engineering firms, subcontractors, the Associated General Contractors and the Associated Builders and Contractors.

Brent believes a person's emotional intelligence is one of the most important predictors of ultimate success for individuals and companies, and his proven program creates fundamental behavioral shifts in employees, improving their performance and increasing the company's bottom line. Brent is a graduate of the Georgia Institute of Technology, and lives in Atlanta, GA with his wife Andrea and their dog Ginger.

If you wish to contact Brent Darnell concerning this emotional intelligence work –

please visit www.brentdarnell.com
email him at brent@brentdarnell.com
or drop him a line at
Post Office Box 13064
Atlanta, GA 30324

This book and cover were designed
and set into type by
Ed Legum.

The text is Adobe Garamond
brought to life in the digital world
by Robert Slimbach.

The initial caps are set in
Goudy Trajan